WHERE PHARAOHS DWELL

ALSO by PATRICIA CORI

The Sirian Revelations

> Vol. 1: *The Cosmos of Soul: A Wake-Up Call for Humanity*

> Vol. 2: *Atlantis Rising: The Struggle of Darkness and Light*

> Vol. 3: *No More Secrets, No More Lies: A Handbook to Starseed Awakening*

The Starseed Dialogues: Soul Searching the Universe

The Starseed Awakening (Audio CD)

WHERE PHARAOHS DWELL

One Mystic's Journey Through the Gates of Immortality

PATRICIA CORI

North Atlantic Books
Berkeley, California

Published by
North Atlantic Books
P.O. Box 12327
Berkeley, California 94712

Cover photo © istockphoto.com/podgorsek
Cover and book design by Brad Greene
Printed in the United States of America

Where Pharaohs Dwell: One Mystic's Journey Through the Gates of Immortality is sponsored by the Society for the Study of Native Arts and Sciences, a nonprofit educational corporation whose goals are to develop an educational and cross-cultural perspective linking various scientific, social, and artistic fields; to nurture a holistic view of arts, sciences, humanities, and healing; and to publish and distribute literature on the relationship of mind, body, and nature.

North Atlantic Books' publications are available through most bookstores. For further information, visit our Web site at www.northatlanticbooks.com or call 800-733-3000.

Library of Congress Cataloging-in-Publication Data

Cori, Patricia.
   Where Pharaohs dwell : one mystic's journey through the gates of immortality / Patricia Cori.
      p. cm.
   Includes bibliographical references.
   ISBN 978-1-55643-830-1
   1. Parapsychology. 2. Occultism. 3. Egyptology--Miscellanea. 4. Pharaohs--Miscellanea. I. Title.
   BF1040.C63 2009
   133.9--dc22

                                                 2009034754

          1 2 3 4 5 6 7 8 9 SHERIDAN 14 13 12 11 10 09

In memory of my true father, my friend,
my teacher

Abd'El Hakim Awyan

Who became
Osiris
during the writing of this book.
Let his light, his love, and the Wisdom
forever shine
through the Halls of Amenti
and beyond
with the stars

—Where Pharaohs Dwell

Contents

Illustrations

FRAMES IN PHOTOGRAPH SECTION

1 The Ship
    Photo by Patricia Cori
2 The Temple of Hatshepsut
    Photo by Patricia Cori
3 Hathor at Hatshepsut Temple
    Photo by Patricia Cori
4 Amir with Patricia at the Cafeteria
    Photo by Patricia Cori
5 Hakim and Patricia on the Balcony
    Photo by Patricia Cori
6 Karnak at Sunrise
    Photo by Patricia Cori
7 Ptah at the Chapel
    Photo by Patricia Cori
8 Ptah at Abydos
    Photo by Patricia Cori
9 Sekhmet Fire
    Photo by Wolfgang Thom
10 Private Ceremony at the Sphinx
    Photo by Patricia Cori
11 The Key
    Photo by Patricia Cori
12 Horus in the Hills
    Photo by Patricia Cori
13A Ma'at Appears in the Darkness
    Photo by Patricia Cori

Foreword

The background story as to how I was asked to write this foreword to *Where Pharaohs Dwell* is an interesting and very synchronistic story in itself. More than a year ago, I knew very little about Patricia as we had never met. I had heard her name and knew she was the author of several books, but that was about all.

That has significantly changed in the last six months. I have learned that Patricia and I lived in the same town, San Jose, California, for a while; we were in France and Egypt at the same times; and we have had similar experiences with deep connections to the star system of Sirius and crystal skulls. But the most significant connection was my learning that Patricia was also a student of my beloved teacher, Abd'El Hakim Awyan (1926–2008).

Hakim was an Egyptian-born Egyptologist and archeologist, and an indigenous wisdom keeper, who was a master of the oral traditions of his native country. I was a student, colleague, and close friend of Hakim for almost sixteen years (1992–2008). I have written two books—*The Land of Osiris* and *From Light into Darkness: The Evolution of Religion in Ancient Egypt*—based on my work with Hakim and my own research for more than forty years.

Together, Hakim and I created a new discipline, *Khemitology,* to differ from the outdated and inaccurate paradigms of academic Egyptology, which we defined as being basically Greco-Roman mythology. I will be writing a third book continuing the work I did with Hakim over the last few years—my final written testament and memorial to this great Master.

Hakim passed over, or as he would term it, "journeyed to the West," on August 23, 2008. After I had sent out the news over the Internet—my group passed the news on to their groups, who passed it on to their groups, etc.—I personally received condolences from hundreds of people from all over the world. One message was from Patricia Cori in Italy, who had been aware of me and my work with Hakim.

The message from Patricia, in loving memory of our beloved teacher, began the friendship and collaboration now present. Patricia was the first person to interview me after Hakim's passing, and it was a powerful and emotional experience for us both. We discussed that Hakim had presented to me the concept of *Khemit*, the ancients' term for their civilization, not Egypt, which was based on the Greek term *Aegyptos*. Hakim taught us that there was a prehistoric, advanced civilization existing in Africa tens of thousands of years before the so-called "dynastic" periods recognized by Egyptologists as being the "only" ancient Egyptian civilization.

These ancient Khemitians, advanced not only technologically but spiritually too, carved the Sphinx as an aspect of the Great Mother, and constructed the stone masonry pyramids we find in various states of ruin in Egypt today. Hakim was adamant that the ancient pyramids were never originally intended to be tombs for any king, or anyone, but were energy devices as elucidated by my colleague, engineer Chris Dunn, in his landmark book, *The Giza Power Plant*.

I now know that Hakim was aware for several years that his time on this physical plane was coming to an end—as early as 2003. A true Master, he selected several students and planted seeds in us to sprout when he would no longer be in the physical.

Because of her unique intuitive abilities and academic background in languages (Hakim was the most profound master of linguistics I have ever experienced), Patricia was one that Hakim knew would appreciate and recognize the timeless wisdom and seemingly endless knowledge that he could share with her. He also most certainly planned for all of us who were his students to come together in his memory and continue his great work. Patricia has become one of the most tireless and dedicated persons to bring in the New Dawn of consciousness that Hakim called the **Awakening.**

We are his spiritual children.

Patricia Cori has written a fascinating and interesting book as part of her contribution to this grand human experience now unfolding. Drawing on her own powerful experiences and strong intuitions with an easy flowing literary style, she presents a real page-turner that one will not want to put down once started. Patricia takes the reader on her personal and unique journey to reclaim a "part" of herself—that being her profound connection to "dynastic" and prehistoric Khemit, the Mother of Civilizations.

It is her open and explicit descriptions of her personal impressions and experiences during several trips to Egypt that have the most interest to me. Having been involved with tours to Egypt since 1992, and having led tours myself since 1998, I have had many amazing experiences personally, and have witnessed profound life-changing and fulfilling instances among those I have brought to Egypt, especially for some women.

Patricia's experiences described in detail in the following pages are among the most incredible and extraordinary that I have ever learned about.

One event and experience in particular (I will not go into detail in order for the reader to fully appreciate it) profoundly moved and affected me. Patricia Cori, as a Western non-Moslem woman, deals with Egyptian Moslem men in this event in a divine moment of inspiration and action-nonaction, which must be reread several times to fully appreciate her courage, wisdom, and the magnificence of that experience.

So, be prepared to ride along on Patricia's journey of self-exploration to find a part of herself in ancient Khemit—a journey of love, laughter, joy, wonder, and the profound wisdom she discovered from my beloved Hakim, from Khemit, and from within herself.

It is a journey I highly recommend and well worth the time and effort.

—Stephen S. Mehler, MA
Lafayette, Colorado
April 25, 2009

∿ 1

The Regression

Back in 1990, well before I had ever read anything significant about Egypt and having never visited the country, I went to a respected past-life regressionist for my very first experience in this now popular form of psychic self-exploration.

A fully credentialed, practicing psychologist, he came highly recommended to me by a dear friend, who had been able to release the torment of some inner demons under his care. She was so enthralled by her experiences and the deep healing process that came from her discoveries through those sessions that she convinced me to book myself an appointment and an airline ticket to Boston to see for myself. Six months later, I went to see him—more out of curiosity, I told myself, than a need for healing.

Then again, I do believe that our desire to unveil our past incarnations is driven by that need, as, in the final outcome, it is the soul's purpose to banish the darkness of repressed memories, so that we can release the karmic chains of old . . . to hasten our way along the path to illumination and to live happier, fuller lives.

My first impression validated my friend's endorsement of this powerful healer and I had no difficulty whatsoever letting go of any anxiety or expectation I had held about him, or the session upon which I was about to embark. After very few preliminaries, I felt calm, relaxed, and ready to be guided to whatever was there for me . . . buried, perhaps, in the deep well of the subconscious, awaiting discovery.

Mesmerized by his hypnotic voice, I quickly let go of the distractions of my chattering mind, noticing how dogs barking outside his studio and the background noise of a telephone in the next room slowly began to fade out of my conscious awareness . . . and how wonderfully relaxed I felt: sinking into his overstuffed reclining chair, letting go to the experience.

I was able to follow his suggestions without distraction, drifting along the currents of his voice, at peace with the world. I could hear the sound of deep inner silence, the riotous voice of resistance slowly giving way to the theta waves of quieted mind.

As he guided me to imagine myself outside of my body, floating in sacred space, I instantly saw before me a beautiful blue eye. It was the color of purest turquoise, but translucent—as were (one can only imagine) the crystal clear waters of ancient shores.

He asked me to identify it: was this the eye of a human being I was looking at, or did it represent some other life form?

No, I saw so clearly that it was a symbol, something like a richly glazed ceramic effigy of an eye: definitely not human, definitely not alive. Later, I would realize that I had been staring into the all-seeing "eye of Horus" of Egyptian lore.

The eye vanished shortly after it had appeared in my vision

and I was catapulted into a hologram of spinning wheels—appearing first as cogs of some great machine, and then morphing into spirals of brilliantly luminous galaxies.

For a fleeting moment, I hovered somewhere far beyond, in deep space, bathed in the twinkling light of so many stars. I became that light—pure starlight—interacting with the galactic fires that surrounded me as conscious, living beings. Celestial music flowed through all that existed, reflecting the soul essence of every star in the heavens and all was perfectly, magnificently "One."

All was resplendent in spirit and the light of consciousness and I was filled with that sense of "total connection" to all that exists—the infinite and inseparable Oneness of Creation. I could hear the Music of the Spheres, playing the sounds of every living being, strumming softly the vibrational strings of the Akashic Record. It was truly a moment of enlightenment, in every sense.

I abandoned myself to the awe-filled experience, only to find myself suddenly jerked from the state of bliss and sucked violently into the center of a tumultuous whirlpool. I began spinning around and around, uncontrollably, becoming more and more dizzy until I finally shouted out that I was going to be sick if I didn't break loose and find my way back out into free space.

From the ecstasy of communing with the light and dancing to the music of the stars, I was thrown into a state of extreme disorientation and fear: utter separation. Nausea rising in my throat, I felt as if I were clinging to nowhere and nothing—spinning into oblivion.

I called out desperately for help. The therapist finally guided me to slow the whirling vortex and to direct my mind to where I would find myself when it came to a full stop.

To my amazement, the spinning ceased, almost as immediately as it had begun.

The celestial canopy was gone.

Now I was looking at the entrance to a mine—a mineshaft. The outside was formed of roughly hewn rock, and plain wooden bars framed the opening. The regressionist pressed me to describe everything within my field of vision, but there wasn't much else there that I could make out with any detail.

I was uncomfortably alone—somewhere—in a remote desert scene. I could feel the sun burning down on my skin and I could hear the wind whipping across the sand. My feet felt as if they were on fire. All that I could see clearly, however, was the opening of this eerie mineshaft.

He guided me to move in closer, so that I could get a look inside the space, but I told him I couldn't . . . I didn't want to . . . I wasn't able to move any closer, as if I were emotionally and physically paralyzed. I could only look from my vantage point, a safe distance away, and all I saw beyond the opening was absolute, impenetrable darkness.

It was not a place I intended to explore—of this, I was certain.

Then, suddenly, the image mutated into one that appeared to be an entrance to a tomb, with some sort of Egyptian-looking hieroglyphs carved onto smooth, white limestone walls. There was the eye again (the blue eye I had seen while floating God knows where), staring back at me, from the wall to the right of the portico.

I gazed upon the mind screen of my visions, trying to get a clearer impression of what was there . . . what I was really seeing. Yes, it was a tomb—clearly Egyptian. There was a rather oddly adorned, masked male figure (was it a guard?) wearing an ornate crown, standing to the left side of the entrance. He held a long wooden rod, rigidly, out to his side, as if guarding the entrance—and here again, all I could see of the inside, beyond him, was darkness.

Again, the therapist directed me to go into the space to observe what it was that my subconscious mind had brought me to see. I could feel the fear racing through my legs and into my upper body like an electric shockwave and I refused to approach the space in any way.

I had no desire, I told him, to see what lurked there.

During what felt like an eternity, the images shifted back and forth: the mineshaft, the tomb entrance—the shaft, the tomb, the shaft again. There was a growing sense of foreboding and discomfort and I wanted to flee the scene, but I couldn't face a return to the turbulence of those spinning wheels and somehow I knew that they were my only way out.

It was then that I felt someone pushing me from behind.

Let me be clear about this—I felt someone physically pushing me, as if from behind the chair, and I wanted to turn around and look to see who was there, but I couldn't move or open my eyes. I was detached from my physical body, yet aware of it at the same time!

In that moment, I realized I truly had achieved some heretofore unknown form of altered consciousness—uncharted space—whereby I was just as aware of being in the state as I was of being in the body: something akin to lucid dreaming, without the dream.

As I contemplated this bizarre state of bi-location, I became frightfully aware that someone or something utterly menacing was intent upon pushing me into this dark void. Was it a mineshaft? Was it a tomb? I couldn't make it out! As the pressure increased, my heart began pounding wildly from the surge of adrenaline racing through my body: the primordial survival instinct.

I adamantly refused to be thrust into the entrance, yet I knew I was powerless to stop it. In that "dark night" of my soul, I was being forced into what was definitively the opening of a tomb, horrified at the realization that the tomb was, in fact, mine.

I got a close enough look at the guard to recognize him as an Egyptian icon—but I had no idea who he might represent. The regressionist told me to ask him who he was and what he wanted to communicate to me, but I knew I could not.

I could not ask—he could not answer. It was somehow written in the ancient record, glowing dimly in the shadows.

He remained expressionless, like a statue: lifeless. We never made eye contact.

The therapist asked me if I had a name. I stumbled over unfamiliar sounds, so difficult to pronounce: "Hat ... et ... Hatshet ... Hatet-sesheti."

Yes, that was the name: Hatetsesheti.

He asked me who this person was and why the name was important, but I couldn't find an answer.

I was totally concerned about the pressure against my back and the terror that someone was intent upon thrusting me into the darkness.

He asked me to observe who it was. Who was trying to push me through the entranceway?

I could not make out a form. All I could see was the shadow of death, and the all-consuming darkness that now had begun to envelop me. His voice soon faded into oblivion, isolating me in remote landscapes of my mind, until finally I realized I wasn't even listening to him anymore.

Or was it that I had gone so deep and so distant that I simply couldn't hear him?

Filled with despair, I began uttering the word "Maatara ... Maatara ... Maatara." I shouted it into the blackness, crying out for my life, until all that was left of my voice was a dull whisper ... and still, I pleaded: "Maatara, why do you forsake me?"

I heard the regressionist's faraway voice, ever fainter, trying to reach me.

"Who is it?" he demanded. "Who is Maatara . . . **Who is Maatara?**"

The crashing sound of a great door closing echoed grimly through my mind and I found myself in absolute darkness— panicking. Voiceless, I still screamed in desperation to be saved. Running my delicate hands over the rough stone walls, I groped my way through the void, desperately searching for a crack ... a crevice ... a way out.

Hopelessly, I beat my fists on the door until all I could feel was the hot, sticky sensation of my own blood oozing over my pulse and trickling down onto my arms.

The distant voice of the regressionist still managed to penetrate the vacuum of my black prison, but it was muffled ... almost imperceptible. I was trapped somewhere so deep within my mind that he could no longer reach me to help me through it. He was trying to tell me there was something there that I had come to see and that it was safe to look, guiding me to observe myself in the space and to examine everything around me.

Safe? I was anything but safe in this dungeon of death. There was only the black terror of the darkest destiny and I knew I was going to have to face it, alone.

The despair and panic were overtaken by a sense of abandonment and immense sorrow...then slow resignation.

I began to hyperventilate, barely managing to breathe.

As the sense of suffocation overcame me, the therapist, concerned that the manifestation of these clearly overwhelming emotions was actually endangering me, both mentally and physically, had no recourse but to guide me away from the distressing scene.

He finally managed to direct me out of the trauma of the regression and back to the safety of "home."

When I returned fully from this intense and deeply disturbing state of altered awareness, I knew, without a question of a doubt, that I had died buried alive in a tomb somewhere, at some very distant place and time, in the ancient lands of Egypt.

Ironically, it is there, in the terrifying darkness of my ancient Egyptian tomb—at my death—where my story begins. . . .

2

Finding Hatetsesheti

This startling and unexpected experience with the regressionist left me, to say the least, extremely bewildered. I felt physically and mentally drained for days and my dreams were all nightmarish reminders of what I had put myself through, in what had been a thoroughly exhausting and utterly traumatic past life and death review.

Days, even weeks later, I was still running the images around and around in my head, always asking myself the questions: Had my mind simply invented this terrifying Egyptian death scene? And to what end?

I have never experienced any extreme manifestation of claustrophobia, which would surely have revealed itself by now, considering my adventurous lifestyle, in and out of pyramids and other tight squeezes around the world. Neither have I ever felt afraid of the dark . . . at least, as far as I can recall, I have never needed to sleep with a light on. If anything, I have always welcomed the cool of the night and the quiet hours, when the world slows down and silence guides the soul to its dream journeys.

You would think that a subconscious memory of death by suffocation, buried alive in an Egyptian tomb, would be terrifying enough to trigger some sort of modern-day psychosis, wouldn't you?

~

We all know how easy it is to trick the mind into embracing an illusion and then to record it as reality, and I am wary...so wary of the ego. We seem to rewrite our own history at every juncture, enhancing the experiences of our lives for the gratification of the insatiable ego-self, which, unresolved, demands constant feeding.

Always aware of how it glorifies the memory and "rewrites" history, I am especially careful to record my experiences meticulously, trying never to enlarge the sensations and events of my rich journey through this lifetime, so that my reference in recalling these is as close to pure truth as is the candle to the flame.

I do my best to always be a critical observer of my own process, knowing that the psychic experience is so utterly subjective that, as a clairvoyant, I continually walk a fine line between credibility and fantasy in my own mind, as well as in the minds of others.

Here, though, there was no "appetizer" for the insatiable ego. There was no glamour of past life glory—something upon which the ego could feast. I was not fantasizing about a lifetime as Cleopatra or Nefertiti, those hackneyed icons of feminine beauty and power. No, this was a dark, dark place filled with insurmountable terror and pain, and it seemed that now that I had brought it up into my conscious experience, it was either going to cling to me like a mummy's sheath, or I was going to cast it off forever.

I began to search for information—anything that could help me unveil the mystery of the disquieting experience that had surfaced from the deep well of my subconscious. I hoped that somewhere in the great archeological libraries of the past there might be a record of these names—names that I had heard so distinctly: "Hatetsesheti" and "Maatara." I felt compelled to find them, knowing, at the absolute core level, that a greater truth would be revealed to me once I did . . . and that somewhere, in the Egyptian landscape of timeless space, a fragment of my soul had gone lost, but not forgotten.

This experience had been so complex and so real to me that I could only believe that somehow, I would find the proof that "Hatetsesheti" and "Maatara" had actually walked the ancient sands of Egypt . . . and that they had been real, live people. These names just had to exist somewhere, buried in an obscure text, perhaps, or hidden, who knows . . . depicted in hieroglyphs, upon some ancient papyrus or temple wall.

As powerful as this process had been for me, I had to have validation that the experience had a reference point in "reality" (whatever that is) and I was determined, almost obsessed, to find it.

I set out to discover some trace of Hatetsesheti at a time when reference materials and books on Egypt were far more scarce— before the Internet, with its vast wealth of information, so readily accessible. I was further limited by the fact that I live in Italy, which still provides very little in the way of English language books and research material.

After my dwindling library resources and investigative attempts revealed nothing, I eventually began to lose interest in what had been for me a truly monumental experience, and fortunately, the impact of the regression—and the trauma that had surfaced through it—slowly began to fade into the background of my busy mind. There, it settled deeply back into the reflecting pool of the soul, where it had lain dormant for who knows how many millennia . . . how many lifetimes.

For a while, I lost interest in the past life memory altogether, yielding to far more powerful messages, which began streaming into my fields of consciousness in 1996, after my first transcendental crop circle experience in the amazing crop formation that came down at Stonehenge that year.

These, telepathic messages sourced from a higher dimension, resulted in a trilogy of channeled books—The Sirian Revelations. They have everything to do with my Egyptian experiences, as I was to learn very quickly after a sequence of events and discoveries brought me into constant and deepening awareness of the secret mysteries of ancient Egypt and their deep connection to the star system of Sirius.

However, like the phoenix, the questions that had been raised by the powerful regression were there, dormant, awaiting the time of renewal. I recorded those extraordinary impressions in my journal and, as best as I could, put the matter of Hatetsesheti and Maatara to rest.

That first visit to Egypt in November of 1997 finally came about after three attempts to visit the land of the pharaohs had, for one reason or another, never materialized and I had resigned myself that there had to be some higher purpose to the obstruction that had been preventing me from making the trip.

Many people experience a common phenomenon of being inexplicably blocked, for one reason or another, from a planned journey to this ancient world. I do believe, without a doubt, that Egypt is so powerful for those seeking a deep, transformational experience that getting there is, of itself, an initiation. Only when you are strong enough and unconditionally prepared for what it will bring into your life do the doors open—as they most certainly did for me that fall.

On that occasion, I had been invited to conduct a workshop in advanced crystal healing for a group of expats living in Cairo, to be held in a private home in the city's wealthy Maadi district, where many foreigners reside. In those first two days in Egypt, I saw nothing but the airport, the most insane traffic in the history of the human race, and the inside of those four walls, where I was a hosted guest during the intensive two days of teaching.

The course completed, I had planned the visit to Luxor, to see the Valley of the Kings and Queens and then to treat myself to a Nile cruise, to visit the primary temples included in the popular itineraries.

Tragically, just one day after my arrival in Cairo, one of the most important of these, the Temple at Deir el-Bahri, had become the gruesome setting of one of the most macabre terrorist attacks ever to occur in Egypt... and one that changed many things in Egypt, just as dramatically as 9/11 changed life in the United States.

The world was horrified by the slaughter of innocent tourists right there, inside the temple walls, and we can still recall the repercussions this event had on tourism to the country then, as they still affect the way things are organized now.

Understandably, the area was officially closed off to tourists, and all foreign embassies posted warnings to their citizens to avoid Luxor completely. The global community was in shock over what had happened there, and Egypt was in deep mourning. Regretfully, I canceled my Nile cruise and shifted my attention to a full-immersion experience of Cairo.

At that time, days after the attack, Egypt was on red alert at every point of access (airports, train stations, ports), with particular attention to primary tourist areas. Armed guards surrounded the Egyptian museum and all the monuments—although, from what I could see, there were very few foreigners around to guard. In fact, looking back, I don't recall seeing any tourists in the streets of Cairo.

A cloud of collective gloom hovered, like dense fog, over the human spirit.

Through a person I met in the crystal healing workshop, I was presented with the opportunity to visit the Sphinx and to get inside the Great Pyramid, alone, in the early hours of dawn. It was, of course, "strictly forbidden," but with the proper amount of baksheesh (the "almighty buck," as we say), nothing is "strictly" anything in Egypt.

The laws are, shall we say, open to "interpretation."

Considering the intensity of heightened security at all the sites, I was surprised to be offered this epic chance to actually touch the mighty arms of the Sphinx, out of reach to tourists, and to enter the pyramid alone.

I wondered how safe and how sane it would be for me to attempt illegal entry into the most important monuments in Egypt, only two days after the worst terrorist attack in Egypt. Then again, reflecting on it, I realized that there might never be a better opportunity than this, simply because there **were** no tourists. The guards would welcome the opportunity to recover lost tips! It just made sense to take the leap and to trust that I would be surrounded in divine light, crawling around the Giza Plateau in the moonlight with an unauthorized, local guide and pockets full of money for those open, waiting hands.

I committed, knowing I would be protected, and certain my life path had led me to the moment for important reasons that, clearly, were still a mystery to me then.

Only those of you who have been to Egypt know the impact of that very first time you stand before the Great Pyramid of Giza, astounded at the immensity of the only remaining monument of the original Seven Wonders of the World. Humble and so small, you gaze upon it, feeling its power course through your veins . . . racing through your energy channels, from head to toe.

You know immediately that this is the work of masters, not slaves; you know that everything you have ever read in the history books is mostly fantasy, while everything you have fantasized about is more likely to be the truth.

It simply takes your breath away.

The busloads of tourists and cameras and guides and vendors and the noise of it all fade into oblivion as you walk the sands of Giza, humbled by the magnificence of what has come before you and the recognition of what humankind, at the apex points of its highest societies, can create.

Farther down the pathway, across the heavily guarded sands of Giza, you come upon the magnificent leonine guardian of the pyramids and their secrets: the Great Sphinx. As you gaze upon her enigmatic face, which peers out onto the horizon of so many Sirian risings past, you are drawn eternally into a mystery that clings to the time and place of an ancient civilization, one that pre-dates, by far, the chronological record of our established history.

The face is supposedly that of Cheops, the pharaoh Egyptologists claim built the pyramid, but the story that links the construction of the Sphinx to his reign just doesn't fit. You only have to look at the head on the structure to realize that it is clearly disproportionate to its massive feline body, which most likely resembled a lioness from head to toe in its original form, so many tens of thousands of years prior.

Moreover, she is of the Sirian vibration: a galactic connection that we are only just rediscovering now, at the hour of our reawakening. That connection to the stars of Sirius is an awareness that the ancient Egyptians appear to have openly revered and acknowledged through their gods, their living temples, and the hieroglyphic record.

To have been given the opportunity to lay eyes for the very first time on the Great Sphinx and the pyramids in the silence of the desert night, with only the light of the moon and the bright blue-white star, Sirius, shining the way, was beyond my wildest imaginings. To be there alone, but for my guide and a few innocuous guards who had all been paid to let me live that experience in peace, was to be "in the moment" as I had never been in it before.

It marked the dramatic beginning of my love affair with Egypt, which only grows stronger with every visit, every time my feet touch ground and I feel that ancestral home taking root within me.

That glorious night of my first initiation into the Egyptian mysteries, I approached the mighty Sphinx alone, the threat of terrorists and tourist police paling before the majesty of what lay ahead of me. Unobstructed, I walked past ancient houses in the sleepy village of Nazlet El Samman, stepped onto the sand, passed just out of view of the coerced guard, and quietly walked into her awaiting arms.

My heart racing from anticipation—adrenaline pumping so wildly through my body that I could feel it rising in my throat—I knew I was placing myself in great danger, just as I knew, in every cell of my being, that this was an appointment I had made lifetimes before.

All was ordained.

All was truly in Divine Order.

Egypt was opening the Gates.

I ask you to visualize how it might be, walking in the light of stars and the moon, alone, in the desert night—approaching the magnificent Sphinx in utter silence. What a privilege!

As I entered into this magical space, I was pulled, as if magnetically, to the breastplate, the rose quartz granite stele positioned between her arms, at the heart level. Instinctively, I pressed my back up against this magnificent carving and aligned myself, so that the entire length of my spinal column was in contact with the stone.

Every chakra activated instantaneously and my third eye blasted wide open, kundalini energy racing through me from the base to the crown, more powerfully than if I'd been hit by lightning.

Aware that I had to be sensitive to the dynamics of the situation and the imminent danger of it all, I tried to stay grounded . . . but obviously I could not. The impact of such an explosion of spiritual energy racing through me, right there, alone in the arms of the Sphinx, obliterated any sense of what surrounded me. I surrendered to it, releasing the fear and simply being in that immense energy, activated beyond belief, trusting, knowing I was free to receive what can only be described as the greatest "cosmic tune-up" of my life: kundalini rising in the arms of the Great Sphinx.

I began to hear loud and rhythmic drums, the heartbeat of Gaia. Soon, I was swimming in the open seas of probable realities, lost somewhere between dimensions: on the one hand, seeing myself standing there, pressed up against the heart of the Sphinx; on the other, spinning out into other worlds, other realms of consciousness.

A voice echoed across the desert: "O Helios, open your bow!"

It was as if Shakespeare himself were performing some multidimensional eulogy from the beyond. Again and again, the voice rang from the studded canopy of stars, filling the cool night air: "O Helios, open your bow!"

The meaning was lost to me then, in the delirium of infinite light exploding through every cell of my being, but I was conscious enough to know it was a "coded message," and that I would eventually be capable of deciphering it.

The breastplate, or "stele," is a multidimensional portal through which the initiate can journey through time, through space, through the heavens themselves. It is the ultimate linking point to Sirius, specifically to Satais, the ascended Sirian star (Sirius B), from where we are receiving some of the most significant keys to unlocking the treasure chest of our starseed origins, just as the ancients did, in the land of Osiris.

Looking back upon that incredible experience, I delight at how incredibly fortunate I was to have been provided that crack in the control networks of earth time and space. In that glorious moment, I was enabled to spend all the time I needed in the embrace of the Sirian goddess: time to receive and download the ancestral, secret codes that are embedded in her sandstone heart.

"Time, supreme, to feel the magic of the no-time," I thought to myself as my Egyptian facilitator pulled me, a reluctant time traveler, back to the third dimension.

These multidimensional codes have been imprinted in the waters of my cellular memory, reflecting back to the conscious mind the glory of passing through the stargate, under the watchful eyes of the greatest Sirian effigy to still grace our Earth.

To have known this miracle . . . to have been initiated by the Great Sphinx herself . . . has made all the difference in my wondrous journey into the mysteries of Egypt and beyond . . . to the stars . . . where pharaohs dwell.

～

Dawn arrived that morning as I was drinking the most delicious tea from the most disgustingly dirty cup in the middle of the desert, with my guide and a Bedouin, who had set up a small camp in the sand dunes, not far from the Giza Plateau.

What a travesty that those in power, the politicians and modern-day rulers, continue to build their walls and cages around the mighty monuments of the world (as if these were theirs to possess) in the guise of that all-too-familiar catchphrase: "security."

Back then, there were no walls around Giza, as there are now, and there were no barriers to this wonderful vision, sitting out in the desert, watching the sun rise over the pyramids.

We had gone out on camels, just after my visit with the Sphinx, as we had had to wait until eight in the morning to enter the Great Pyramid and it was safest to take ourselves away from the suspicious eyes of the guards, coming in on the new shift, at their main post directly in front of the Sphinx.

Sitting there, looking out at the pyramids on the horizon, I kept running my hands through the sand in order to ground myself back into the physical realm, through which I was reconnecting with other worlds. To my amazement, a small ceramic effigy of a beetle fell right into my palm—right there, in the middle of the desert! I stared at it in utter disbelief, realizing I had been given a gift of immeasurable significance and a message of far greater importance.

Later, I would learn that to the Egyptians, the scarab symbolized the *Age of Awakening*.

Here I was, I reminded myself over and over again, at the epicenter of the Earth's energy grid network, sipping tea on a dune of Saharan sand. An ancient amulet had fallen into my hand, as if by magic—a harbinger of things to come. Filled with a sense of gratitude and celebration, I reminded myself to stay grounded and connected to the Earth, to the moment, and not delude myself with imaginings of what lay ahead.

I gazed out at the horizon, amused to see only one cloud, which had formed a perfect circle, as if God had blown a cigarette ring into the sky. The rising sun appeared to pass right through it, like a ball passing through a hoop.

"*O Helios*," I reiterated, my mind and heart and soul free of any other moment but that, "*Open your bow . . .*"

How wonderful when we are able to extract ourselves from the madness of our fast-lane worlds to find the time and the space where we can be receptive to such miracles—to experience the outer reaches of universal consciousness. How extraordinary, indeed, when we receive these great gifts, taking ourselves to the power places of the Earth, places where our ancient souls have no doubt passed in some other life context—a place and time with which they still resonate and so long to return to.

First the Sphinx and now, in just a few hours, I would be inside the Great Pyramid of Giza, a privileged explorer, climbing hidden stairways, searching for spiritual treasure.

Alone in the Great Pyramid? It was a lot to ask of myself, I realized. Whatever I would discover inside its mighty, secretive walls, I knew for certain that it was going to be a psychic overload, particularly after what I had just experienced, hours before, at the Sphinx.

I was glad that I had no preconceived ideas about the purpose or design of the great monument, as I always prefer to receive and integrate the right-brained, psychic impressions before the left brain researches, acquires data, and records the information.

To this day I still approach new adventures in this way, limiting what I read or absorb from the experience of others, to glean what I can from my own interaction with the energies that have been woven through time and place. I ask no less of my students and fellow journeyers—those who participate in my workshops and sacred tours. To be open to receive, in the moment, is to allow oneself the possibility of truly life-altering, breakthrough discoveries.

The endless miles of research and hypotheses that line the information highways leading to Egypt (from the wisdom of the ancient Greek scholar Herodotus, to the archeological breakthroughs of our modern-day Egyptologists) can always follow. I believe, however, that as we travel that mysterious and inviting path of spiritual awakening, we are most rewarded when we are unencumbered, intuitive, and receptive to the impressions and experiences we acquire **directly** from the source.

21

These sensitive moments, and the psychic charge that we receive when we live them, are ours and ours alone. Pure and powerful, they are the glue that binds the scattered pieces of an endless puzzle: our long, long journey through many revolutions upon the Great Wheel of Karma and upward, returning to Source, on the Spiral of Light.

∽

Having had no sleep, I returned to Giza at eight a.m., on camelback, and proceeded with my guide to my second checkpoint, at the base of the Great Pyramid, where we waited for the guards to let us in.

I watched as my guide climbed to the entrance to manage the tipping, the "baksheeshing" of the appropriate people, which the Egyptians affectionately refer to as "the left hand out." However, from the animated discussion between them, I could see that something was wrong and that, in fact, the guards had upped the stakes and were asking for more money before any of them would be bringing "the left hand" back in.

This happens, I soon learned, all the time. They haggle, they agree, they haggle again, and on and on until the most that can be squeezed from the one paying is reached and everyone gets his due share, which they perpetually grumble over . . . no matter how satisfied they actually are with the settlement. However, I wasn't willing to spend any more than I had already committed to, well over three hundred dollars, as I didn't have it to give.

The new guard refused. He wanted two hundred dollars more to arrange for me to be absolutely alone for a two-hour visit and there was no moving him from his position.

They managed to reach a compromise: I would be allowed to

go in with a private group that was holding a ceremony in the King's Chamber. They would enter the front passageway and once they had all veered to the right, to climb the stairs leading up to the Grand Gallery, I would sneak in behind them and climb down into the subterranean chamber, which had been my desire from the start.

This was a perfect plan except for one minor detail: there was a gate blocking the tunnel into the chamber and the guards claimed they didn't have the key. This meant I was forced to climb over the gate (no easy feat), breaking more laws, to then begin the excruciating climb down the tunnel, whose ceiling is so low that you pretty much have to make the entire climb bent in half.

At the last leg of this arduous climb, the tunnel becomes very narrow and you can get through only by crawling on all fours, which bears a remarkable similarity to the rebirthing process. I did this, valiantly, without a sign of claustrophobia, even though the idea that I could get stuck in this tight passageway definitely crossed my mind: somewhat humorously at first, followed by a very palpable sense of anxiety.

Once inside the subterranean chamber, or "pit" (as it is called by archeologists), I was overcome with two conflicting sensations. The first was the wonder of being there, feeling the enormity of it all—deep inside the bowels of the Great Pyramid of Giza. The second, taking precedence over the wonder, was the realization that I was way below the exit level of the pyramid, illegally, and that only two people in the entire world knew I was there: my unofficial Egyptian guide and a relatively uncooperative guard . . . one who was still grumbling about more money.

As I always do when I enter high-energy vortices, I closed my eyes and began to meditate, calling upon the angelic realms for protection and guidance, asking that the fear be transmuted into power and that the power be experienced as pure joy. I asked to be encircled in pure white light and that only the highest good be made manifest, calling in my spirit guides, the Ascended Masters, and light beings from the highest realms, whose intention it was to guide my journey.

This is important preparation for any mystical experience and I cannot stress it enough when working with others. These immense vibrations attract every kind of energy, from the darkest forces to the ultimate radiance of Spirit, and we must be so pure in our intent when we approach them.

It is always essential to call in the Warriors of Light before entering the power places of this Earth, just as it is when working on the astral planes and higher dimensions from the comfort of our own, more familiar environments.

As I performed this invocation, huge waves of energy roared through the space, washing over me with immense brilliance. It was then, in that illuminating moment, that I understood the meaning of the words that had echoed across the hollow desert from my Shakespearean messenger: I had been given the key to unlocking the portal—the deep chamber of the Great Pyramid.

"O Helios," I whispered into the penumbra and ancient stone. "Open your bow!"

"O Helios," I repeated in full voice. "Open your bow!"

I opened my eyes to find that a wooden ship had appeared in the shadowy depths of the pit. A majestic female form with a feline head—the head of a lioness—stood tall and regal at the bow and I knew I was supposed to board the ancient vessel to journey with her.

In one of the greatest astral journeys of my life, I stepped over the threshold, surrendering to that moment, to be steered through the limitless waters of the cosmic sea under the loving tutelage of the goddess.

Later, I would learn that she was Sekhmet ("She Who is Powerful"), one of the most revered gods of the Egyptian pantheon … but at the time, all I knew was that this was my ship to other worlds and dimensions and that this majestic goddess was my captain.

The experience of that journey is so very personal and it is filled with incredible visions of which I cannot speak, but I **can** tell you that among these, I was taken to the underworld, the Land of Osiris, and shown just where the Halls of Amenti really lie.

~

The appearance of the Egyptian guide, who had crawled down into the chamber entrance to tell me it was time to leave, broke the trance and I came crashing back into my body, to find myself back in the deep cavern of the Great Pyramid.

Clearly, I was in no condition to start the long and strenuous climb back to the outer world.

I asked him to switch off the lights and leave me in the chamber alone, for only a few more minutes, as I felt I had to experience the darkness to test the information I had retrieved in the past life regression I'd had in Boston.

The lights went out.

To my delight, I felt no panic or breathlessness: only wonder.

Alone, in absolute darkness, deep within the underground cavern beneath the massive Great Pyramid of Giza, I felt only **wonder.**

When the lights were first turned off, I noticed something flash, almost phosphorescent, just next to my foot. I reached down and picked up something that felt like a rock—whatever it was that had sent up that message of light—and, turning to go, I said goodbye to my captain, my guide through the realms of unknown worlds.

I held the rock tightly in my hand as I started back up the grueling climb through the tunnel, which I knew, of course, was going to be more challenging than the climb down. I had to hurry and had no time to inspect the gift that scintillated in my palm.

As energized as I was from what had transpired, it still seemed like the taxing climb would never end. In fact, as I would learn from a later visit, it is far more difficult to climb down to the pit than it is to climb up to the King's Chamber, both tedious for the admittedly unfit (but determined) explorer that I am.

When I finally got outside the Great Pyramid, out of view of the guard, I opened my palm to see what it was that I had been clutching and had brought up from the depths of the subterranean world below. To my surprise, I was holding a limestone carving, however crude, of an ancient Egyptian ship. *See Frame 1 in the color photo section.*

Like the carved beetle from the desert sands, it is one of the most important gifts I have ever received and it is one of the most powerful transporters I have ever worked with in my spiritual journeying.

I have shown my ship to a few archeologists in Egypt, who say it is "nothing." I have even taken it to the British Museum and they, too, claim it is too crude to be "anything of value."

Ah, but to me, it is one of the most valuable of all possessions:

my solar boat, my way of passage through the Duat . . . a gift from the goddess Sekhmet and the keeper gods at the Great Pyramid.

$\sim$

Soon after these remarkable first events in Egypt, a period I always refer to as the "giant leaps phase" of my spiritual and psychic life, I was given the opportunity to return to Egypt, precisely in March of 1998, with far more free time to explore and far more determination to find Hatetsesheti.

I planned for the two-hour wait at the Rome airport with a classic tourists' guidebook, *Egypt: A Phaidon Cultural Guide*. Once past the tedium of check-in and security clearance, I sat down with the book with the intention of finding something, anything, that might trigger some more ancient memories, sunk deep within the reservoir of my subconscious—or buried, somewhere, in the tombs of ancients.

A dowser, I always open books randomly, letting them fall open to me. It is always my uncanny experience that something extremely relevant to that moment is inevitably waiting for me on the page.

I was not disappointed. I had opened to a page that described the Temple of Hatshepsut, about whom I have learned much more in these recent years, but who was still unknown to me then. I was amazed to see that the location of this temple was where the massacre had taken place: the Temple of Deir el-Bahri. It was the temple of the female pharaoh/queen, Hatshepsut, a name that was so very similar to the one I had so long searched for in texts: Hatetsesheti.

I read on. To my amazement, there on that very page was written:

"The raised arms of the Ka, below the uraeus serpent crowned by a sun disk, have been removed from the uppermost frieze, because all of these emblems taken together are a coded version of **Ma'atkare**" *(also spelled Ma'atkara)—Hatshepsut's pharaonic name during her reign.*

"Ma'atkare" in Hieroglyphics

I was astonished! The possibility that both names had found counterparts in this text had to be more than coincidence and that the book had opened to this spot was enough to grab my attention, to say the least. And then, of course, there were those familiar "body chills," racing from my feet up to my scalp, that signal the psychic affirmation, and which are always a sign of truth unfolding.

Surely, the names Ma'atkara and Maatara were close enough to be considered an absolute match (I marveled at the fact that I had even spelled the name almost identically), and even though the name of the Pharaoh Hatshepsut differed from the one that I had heard as my own, Hatetsesheti, it was surely close enough to warrant more investigation.

Completely dumbfounded to have fallen upon this information, I read on in the text to decipher the meaning of the name Ma'atkara.

Ma'at: *The concept of Ma'at depicted as either a goddess with the typical feather in her diadem or the feather alone, includes the entire system of the world. At the judgment of the dead, the heart of the* *deceased is weighed against the Ma'at (the feather) and judgment is passed, based on the divine balance in truth-justice.*

Ka: *The Divine Spirit*

Ra: *The Sun God-Amen.*[1]

Ma'atkara, then, should mean "The Justice of the Divine Spirit of Ra." There, in those last moments of some remote lifetime, with my last breath, I had called out the name *Maatara* until I had no voice left, desperate in the darkness—buried alive. Had I been pleading to the gods for justice, from my tomb, I contemplated, or was I, Hatetsesheti, crying out to my dead pharaoh?

I celebrate synchronicity, always marveling at how things come at the perfect moment across our paths, merging, intersecting, pointing us in the right direction. We are blessed with such divine guidance, constantly and with great eloquence—but all too often we are so distracted by the static hum of our lives that we become entrained by the noise and blind to our messengers.

These are the moments when we miss the proverbial "exit" on the great highway of experience.

When we are receptive and aware, these magnificent harmonies—synchronistic moments—are at the best of times like glorious symphonies . . . at others, like the gentlest of lullabies. When, instead, we are distracted, the musicians still play for us, but, unnoticed, their song seems to fade into the shadows, dissipating in thin air.

---

[1] Marianne Mehling, ed., *Egypt: A Phaidon Cultural Guide* (London: Phaidon Press Limited, 1990).

It is not unlike the philosopher's question: "If a tree falls in the forest, but no one hears it hit the ground, did it ever really happen?"

Tuned in, though, we get the beat. **We get it.** We make sense of how it all plays together, beautiful music: each note a stream of consciousness, playing from the sheet music of life—the space-time continuum; each stream flowing through the rivers of universal mind and reverberating out, into the cosmic sea.

One measure of the messages that spring from the subtle energy fields surrounding and penetrating us is found in numerology. Essentially, numerology is a study of the vibrational essence of the Universe through the archetypal qualities of numbers, which, inevitably, provide us with clues into various aspects of the nature of consciousness.

An elementary departure point for a glimpse at how numerology reflects our personal vibrational essence begins with defining one's soul number, an archetype of the vibration that defines the soul's purpose in this lifetime.

It follows the basic precept that the soul chooses the day and time of birth. It chooses the characters who will form the core group of family and all significant relationships, good and bad, all for a higher purpose: to climb the spiral of the "I am" experience—on our way back to the pure light of Source. That purpose, according to numerologists, is reflected through the soul number and, so, the vibrational frequencies reflected in the numerology of the birth date are tools that the soul consciously chooses to work with in the specific reincarnation.

To arrive at this number, you add the day, month, and year of your physical birth (intended as your emergence from the womb), which will give you a four-digit total (see below). You then add these four digits to arrive at a double digit number—you then reduce this to one digit through addition (unless that double digit is twenty-two, considered a "master" number) to arrive at a single digit number, which, it is believed, holds its own very particular vibrational quality.

To simplify this seemingly confusing process, observe the calculation of a soul number by adding the numerical correspondents of a hypothetical date of birth (December 3, 1951) as follows:

Day	03
Month	12
Year	1951
Total	1966

Having reached this four-digit figure (the total), you now add across: $1 + 9 + 6 + 6 = \mathbf{22}$

In traditional numerology, you would again add the two-digit total (example $2 + 2 = 4$) and that final number would indicate the soul number. However, as indicated above, twenty-two is a special number and it is the exception to the rule.

My personal soul number also totals twenty-two.

This number corresponds to the Fool card in the tarot, as it is the twenty-second card of the major arcana (the primary cards), although the actual number represented on the card is 0. This peculiarity has everything to do with the spiritual essence of the Fool, representative of the Wheel of Karma upon which the soul revolves between the spirit realm and material existence, which in many ways defines its very special attributes.

31

Observing the card closely, you can see that etched upon the sack the Fool carries (attached to a rod) is the eye of Horus. His headpiece is adorned with a great reddish feather at the center, just as the headdress of Ma'at is depicted in Egyptian hieroglyphs.

Interestingly, the Fool card, described in the more ancient European decks, is called *Le Mat*! And here I was, the Fool in my own right, leaping off the proverbial cliff fearlessly, on my way to remembering.

It was the twenty-second of March . . . an important day and I was seated in the twenty-second row of the aircraft. From the numerological perspective, it was clearly the right vibration for a soulquest journey, as it was the vibration that corresponded to my soul's purpose. From astronomical perspectives, it was a time of renewal: Spring Equinox.

After landing in Cairo, I still had to connect to my flight to Luxor, with a two-hour layover between flights. Browsing the airport selection of typical tourist publications, I picked up and began to browse through a guidebook on the Valley of the Kings, which I "fool"ishly did not purchase, so I cannot reference it here, but I did scribble some notes into a long-lost journal, which remain, nonetheless, chiseled on my mind screen, like sculpted granite.

Once again, as in the case back in Rome, I had opened directly to a page that spoke of Pharaoh Hatshepsut. Here was found a listing of the rulers of the New Kingdom, and, not surprisingly, Hatshepsut was the twenty-second name on the list.

The book described Hatshepsut's Eighteenth Dynasty funerary temple and its twenty-two lower portico pillars. According to the text, she ruled twenty-two years.

I remember saying to myself out loud: "Is this enough synchronicity for you, P. Cori?"

∾ 3
Synchronicity

On the west bank of the mighty Nile, across from Luxor, lies the Valley of the Kings, where history has proven many pharaohs chose to be buried in elaborate tombs, most of which have been desecrated, raided for their riches by ancient and modern-day thieves—and then robbed of their spiritual integrity by archeologists and tourists alike.

Eager to finally visit the area after my first visit to Egypt did not allow it, I decided to make my first stop there, in the valley, so that I could explore the rich history and the clues to Egyptian mysticism contained in the tombs at my own pace . . . and then visit the Temple of Hatshepsut.

Somehow, I knew that there I would find keys to my locked memories.

My experience at the tombs was so utterly traumatic that, despite my desire to examine the mysterious glyphs and carvings that adorn those sacred spaces, I have never again felt a desire to return to the hidden chambers of the pharaohs' passings. I just cannot bear to violate the hallowed chambers of ancients and, in that one occasion when I did enter one such showcased landscape of the dead, I felt like an invasive and most unwelcome voyeur.

Above and beyond the difficulty inherent in climbing deep into the burial chambers, with their dank, stifling atmospheres, is the sacrilege of invading what had been created as their ulti- mate temples, from where the souls of the pharaohs believed they would find safe passage through the Duat (the underworld), assuring that their physical bodies would remain immortalized throughout eternity and that their souls would be free to soar far above, to the stars.

These most private of holy places were never meant to be dis- turbed—even less to be reduced, as they are, to the touristic Dis- neyland that they have become.

During that one and only visit to Egypt's pharaonic burial grounds, I developed such a severe case of acute pneumonia that, on my return home from Cairo, I had to be taken directly to the hospital, coughing blood. The attending physician admitted me immediately, after X-rays revealed that more than twenty per- cent of my left lung was covered in dense inflammation (which, coincidentally, he described as a "pyramidal mass"). The progno- sis was that the road to recovery would take weeks, if not months, of total bed rest.

The symptoms were fierce from the onset, marked by intense respiratory difficulty and ceaseless, violent coughing. These had begun, uncannily, just as my van first entered the Valley of Dead Pharaohs.

I could not stop coughing . . . I couldn't catch my breath . . . and I felt deep pain in my lungs from the moment we arrived there. All of these symptoms came on quickly and without warning.

Having made the effort to get myself there, I was not going to let my lungs get in the way of discovery and I pushed myself to explore at least one tomb. Despite the extreme discomfort, I dragged myself up a long and rather steep stairway into one of the oldest of the discovered tombs of the valley—the tomb of Thutmosis III, which I was told was one of the most beautiful of all those open for public viewing.

The inexplicable coughing and choking exacerbated the difficulty of the climb up the outer stairway, leading to the tomb's entrance, which I just barely survived—only to then have to climb down into the outer passageway leading to the main chamber, where the eye is indeed rewarded with fantastic hieroglyphic artworks adorning the walls.

The tomb was crammed with tourists and it was stifling, hot, and unbearable. What little oxygen circulated in the tight space was being sucked into the hungry lungs of us all—irreverent spectators—making it impossible for me to breathe. I tried, but just couldn't stand it and had to rush out of the tomb, literally climbing over people to force my way out, blindly racing to the light.

I stood at the outer entrance, gasping for air and choking with asthma-like symptoms, between the intense bronchial coughs. I wouldn't necessarily call it a case of claustrophobia. It was more like absolute terror.

A few people looked at me, but no one reached out.

Overcome with raging, unrecognizable emotions, and a sense that I was somewhere between the dimensions, I felt distant and out of touch, on the one hand; close and "remembering," on the other.

Recalling that experience, almost all I can remember of the events of that day is the desperation I felt inside the tomb of Thutmosis III, the walls closing in on me, and how I all but beat my way past the clump of tourists to get free, desperately racing to the passageway and out...as if my very life depended upon it, which, no doubt, it did.

Fortunately, what remains central in my mind today is not the torment of that experience, but rather the sweetness of that first breath of oxygen, when I made it out of **that** tomb—alive.

Forsaking the visit to Hatshepsut's temple, I raced back to the comfort of my hotel in Luxor and threw myself into bed, attempting to calm the chaos in my mind and to ease the disharmony in my body. I called for a doctor, yielding to modern medicine for a dose of life-saving antibiotics and, begrudgingly, dedicating the next few days to absolute bed rest—doctor's orders.

The two feverish nights I spent there were a brutal brew of nightmares and ceaseless coughing fits—both symptomatic of my hellish experience in the tomb of Thutmosis.

After those two forgettable days, I felt stronger and I was determined to forge on, to see what I had come to see—and so I hired a driver and organized a private visit to the amazing Temple of Hatshepsut at Deir el-Bahri. *See Frame 2.*

One of Egypt's most celebrated archeological masterpieces, this remarkable temple was known as "Djeser Djeseru," the most magnificent of the magnificent. Designed by Senenmut, the Royal Vizier and the man believed to be Hatshepsut's secret lover, it was revered as the most magnificent of all royal temples, throughout time. It is, indeed, a breathtaking monument to the one historians refer to as the "first female pharaoh." Her reign was fraught with intense rivalry from her stepson, Thutmosis III, who, I believe, murdered her twenty-two years after the start of her rule as one of the greatest pharaohs of Egypt.

What kind of amazing synchronicity was it, I wondered, that

had pulled me into his very tomb in that frightful experience days earlier? Coincidence? I don't think so. I can't help but believe that I was meant to feel that rage, to reexperience a trauma that later I would discover was linked to him, as an integral part of my pulling together the bits and pieces of my scattered memories of that remarkable time.

I am convinced that he murdered Hatshepsut and that he destroyed almost all symbols and effigies of her from the temple walls of all of Egypt.

He spit on her dead body, before he acquiesced to the priests who insisted that, as pharaoh, she must, at the very least, be mummified before burial.

You can feel his hatred in the air at Deir el-Bahri.

You can see it with your inner vision and sense it on your skin.

And you can see his destruction of Hatshepsut's memory everywhere around you.

Back in March of 1998, there were still very few tourists coming to the site, since the attack four months prior was still fresh in everyone's minds. Because of that, I was able to find the beloved silence I always seek in sacred space as I walked from pillar to pillar, tuning in psychically, enjoying the rare freedom from noise and disturbance.

As I walked the weathered stones of ancient times, asking that the hidden be revealed to me, I kept thinking that the blaze of burning sunlight was blocking my inner eye and making me so uncomfortable in my own skin. I would have liked to stay there until nightfall: to walk through the temple in the cool of night, in the moonlight; to listen, perhaps, for the whisper of ancient spirits; to awaken my own ancient memories.

Someone or something seemed to hear that thought and decided to respond to it.

As I entered the sacred halls of the Hathor Chapel, off to the left of the temple complex, I heard a voice—something I can describe only as "otherworldly"—like that which I had heard at Giza. I looked around for the speaker but, to my surprise, I found I was alone in the chapel at that moment. The rest of the tourists, however few and far between, were scattered at other locations inside the grounds.

Clearly and distinctly, just as real and discernible as any mortal sound could be to the ear, I heard the words: *"Hatetsesheti, O devoted one,"* a woman's voice resounded through the temple walls, *"do not grieve for me . . ."*

I spun around, freaked out, knocking my camera from the ledge where it rested. As it crashed to the ground, ancient memories raced again through my head, washing over my soul. I burst into tears with a vengeance, sobbing deeply in the middle of Ma'atkara's sacred walls, imploring the goddess Hathor . . . for what, I did not know.

Again, the voice echoed through the porticos: *"You can find me in the stars, for it is here I dwell, where men move as gods."*

I looked around frantically, searching for that "something" . . . that "someone," while the penetrating eyes of the Hathor goddess, overhead, silently pierced the still air of the valley. *See Frame 3.*

I remember thinking that the gift of psychic vision can truly be a double-edged sword: one that opens you to incredible experiences, yes, but at the same time has you perennially questioning them, forever seeking to separate fantasy from reality, as you walk the very thin line that exists between the realms.

Thankful that no one had been around to see me go through this, I pulled myself together as best I could and reached down to pick up my shattered camera. I was intrigued to see a desert beetle, the Egyptian symbol of the awakening, inching its way out of a small opening in the stone pavement.

"They don't come out in the heat of day," I mused, knowing this symbol was clearly important, having appeared to me a second time from the earth of Egypt.

It came boldly into the excruciating sun and crossed just in front of my left foot. There it stopped, turned around decisively, and, just as quickly as it had appeared before me, raced back to the cool of its hidden world.

Divine messengers are all around us, existing between the layers of our material world and the subtle fabric of other realities: the voice, the beetle, and the memory all representations of the threads of some incredible, multidimensional tapestry that is being woven through time and space, perpetually, through many lifetimes. We spin the cosmic tale of our own existence, soul moving higher, life and death dancing us through our perennial return upon the cosmic wheel of reincarnation.

We are blessed to be reflections of that greater intelligence that we know, on some level, directs the Cosmos. When we attune to its pulse (the nuances of the elements, our minds, the living beings around us), we begin to unravel the secrets of our own magnificent past: from seed, to being, to race, to species, to starseed of worlds far beyond our own. From there, we imagine our future selves, extensions beyond this density, when we return to the stars and eventually find our way back to the All-Encompassing Light.

One great lesson I have learned is to pay attention to the seemingly small things—the desert beetle—rather than forever distracting myself with expectations of great awakenings and the pressing desire for spiritual epiphanies.

Those come soon enough, when we are ready—when we are truly living and speaking our absolute truth.

They come when we have earned them . . . and only then.

Everything else, it seems to me, is the illusion of our own egos playing the banjo, not the harp, in our minds.

∾ 4
Omm Sety

After visiting Hatshepsut's temple, I yielded to my body messages of weakness and fatigue and grabbed a flight back from Luxor to Cairo, cutting my Egypt stay short. I just didn't have the strength to do more. Waiting for my connecting flight home at the airport in Cairo, I distracted myself with last-minute window-shopping at the few gift shops there were then—back before the modernization of the international terminal. I searched the bookstand, hoping to find the guidebook on the Valley of the Kings, but it was out of stock. What I did find, instead, was a book that would add a new layer to my growing Egyptian experience: *The Search for Omm Sety*[2] by author Jonathan Cott.

From the front cover, the book first appeared to be some sort of intriguing mystery/romance novel, but as I read the back cover as well I realized I was staring at yet another amazing synchronicity in my unfolding Egyptian mystery.

The text read: *"The Search for Omm Sety is a transfixing account of psychic phenomena, astral travel and materialization—the two worlds of Dorothy Eady ... a remarkable woman and her self-declared reincarnation."*

---

[2]Jonathan Cott, *The Search for Omm Sety* (London: Arrow Books Ltd., 1989).

I remember thinking how out of place a book about an English-woman's reincarnation seemed, nestled in among a bunch of classically commercial travel guides at an airport bookstore in Cairo (of all places). I felt intrigued by it, certain that this book about a woman discovering a past life in ancient Egypt was meant for me, as it fit so perfectly with what was unfolding in my own life.

Excitedly, I gathered up all my grubby Egyptian pounds to find I had just exactly enough to buy the book, sensing that it would turn out to be a coalescing thread in my golden cord to Egypt. In fact, it was the key to another whole chapter in my awakening memory of past lives in the land of gods and pharaohs. It would soon mark the beginning of a journey that would take me deep into the greater mysteries of the land of Ur, the Egypt of the Khemitians—those tribes that claimed sovereignty of the Saharan lands well before the first pharaohs appeared.

Omm Sety, an incredible woman with a most intriguing life story, would speak to me from between the lines.

From the minute I opened the book and began to read its first pages, I recognized that another messenger, with a new piece of an ancient story, had led me to her.

There, on the first page, I found the author had chosen this quote as his introduction to the book:

Remind me again—together we
trace our strange journey, find
each other, come on laughing.
Some time we'll cross where life
ends. We'll both look back

as far as forever, that first day.
I'll touch you—a new world then.
Stars will move a different way
We'll both end. We'll both begin.
Remind me again.

> —"Our Story"
> (From *Stories That Could Be True* by William Stafford)

Of stars moving "a different way," I knew immediately that I was being reminded of the message I had heard at the Hathor Chapel at Deir el-Bahri, *"You can find me in the stars ... for it is here I dwell ... where men move as gods."*

Prophetically, the piece was quoted, according to the text, from *Stories That Could Be True.*

The story of Omm Sety is one of a charmingly eccentric Englishwoman, Dorothy Eady, and her absolutely remarkable life, which ended in 1981, when she passed from her earthly life as the caretaker of the Temple of Abydos to join her great love, Pharaoh Sety I, in the afterlife.

Her rediscovery of another lifetime so many thousands of years before is beautifully recounted in the book. Through it, we learn how, at a very early age in her conservative British upbringing, the young Dorothy began to experience visitations from the handsome ghost of her former love, Pharaoh Sety I, with whom she later came to believe she had shared a tragic life in the Temple of Abydos, in Egypt.

From the time of these first ghostly visits and throughout her lifetime, filled with so many years of encounters with the spirit of the pharaoh, she had been capable of vividly recalling her lifetime as the young, virginal Priestess Bentreshyt of Abydos. There, in the constraints of forbidden love, Pharaoh Sety I fell in love with her during his visits to the temple's construction site, where, history has it, he had decided to build the greatest treasury to his own spirit, in worship of the gods of the pantheon. Some sources believe the temple was there long before Sety came in and renovated it.

Through the pages of the book, Cott recounts Omm Sety's incredible story of two immortalized lovers who, blinded by passion, commit the ultimate sin of consummate love, shaming them both before the priesthood and damning them to what she believed to have been "the wrath of the gods."

This act of passion results in the unthinkable pregnancy, for which she, Bentreshyt, is cast out from the temple and commits suicide, condemning both souls to eternal separation in the afterlife. Many millennia later, Pharaoh Sety returns to her in spirit form, calling her back to their sacred Temple of Abydos, to heal the karma of their acts, and to prepare the way for their souls to be reunited.

It would actually read as a new age Cinderella story, were it not for the fact that Dorothy Eady eventually moved to Egypt, married and had a son there, and after years of working for the Department of Antiquities in Cairo, managed to get herself assigned to the remote village of Abydos.

Her innate knowledge of Egypt and its history was unprecedented, they found, and even the most renowned Egyptologists of the time were stunned to find that, with relative ease, the foreign woman could read hieroglyphs that had never before been deciphered. She would locate and identify undiscovered sites to archeologists that, when excavated, would turn out to be exactly as she described. In short, she proved herself a formidable Egyptologist in her own right and demonstrated, time and time again, that she knew the sacred temple of Sety I and all its magic, to which she devoted her life, better than any other modern historian—dead or alive.

She was so incredibly gifted and uncannily knowledgeable in Egyptian history that even the hierarchy of male "lords" of the Department of Antiquities yielded to her knowledge. They hired her, the first woman ever to work for the Department, to decipher the indecipherable, decoding reams of text that had lain in darkness for so many thousands of years, before she read them into the light of modern interpretation.

This blonde haired, unconventional woman lived out her life in a humble mud hut in Abydos, near the temple grounds. Hers was a lifetime dedicated to recording and restoring the exquisite Holy Temple of Sety I, a place where she believed she had died, thousands of years prior, in shame and disgrace, severed from the gods. It was the place where her twin flame, Pharaoh Sety I, had returned from the underworld to guide her through the Halls of Amenti and back to the Elysian Fields of eternal life, sacrificing his place in the stars for the light of his twin flame and soul mate, Bentreshyt.

I was so mystified by what I read in those first pages that I actually considered canceling my flight home to head to this place, Abydos—but my body was screaming for me to get home for medical care.

I yielded to the so-called "adult within" and went home, thoughts of Omm Sety and Abydos swirling around in my head like the galaxies that had had me spinning during the regression—symbols of the wheel of return upon which I have journeyed so many lifetimes before.

It wasn't until Spring of 2001 that I finally managed to visit Abydos for the first time. In the years between my visits to Egypt, I had been taken on a far different journey—a voyage of the mind and soul—connecting with that incredible hyperspace intelligence that identified itself as the "Speakers of the Sirian High Council." The process of bringing through their messages in my earlier books and getting them published, all within a four-year period, required incredible focus and commitment and so, during that time, I did not stray far from the keyboard and my busy life in Rome.

The books birthed and on their way, I was able to return to my passion for Egypt, knowing there was so much awaiting me in her sacred halls—especially within those sacred walls of the temple at Abydos.

The most holy city of ancient worship, Abydos is, to this day, relatively obscure, like hidden treasure, nestled between the harsh desert sands of the Sahara on one side and the rich and fertile Nile banks on the other. It lies situated in a sun-drenched haven, where the mountain ridge opens, like a stairwell, to allow the sun god, Ra, to descend into Earth's embrace.

Here are found Omm Sety's beloved Temple of Sety I and the mysterious Osireion, the indecipherable and far more ancient lower temple complex, believed to be the possible burial place of the god Osiris, Lord of the Underworld. Other temple ruins line the horizon and it turns out the desert is, in fact, an immense burial ground for those ancient worshippers of Osiris, whose dream it was to be buried near the megalithic structure, believed to be his actual burial temple.

This utterly incredible place has lured true seekers from time immemorial, for it is the Mecca of all ages—the Holy of Holies.

Fortunately, for all the ancient souls who still rest, undisturbed, in the sacred fields of the true land of Osiris, Abydos is still relatively "off the radar" to mass tourism, protected by the gods perhaps, remote enough that only determined pilgrims and a limited number of seekers take the extra time and travel the distance to visit there.

And that is a good thing . . . a very good thing indeed.

Because of the terrorist attack in Luxor in 1997, travel inland to the more remote areas of Abydos and the nearby temple of Dendera required traveling by convoy with police escorts then, as it still does today, and getting myself there was going to be a feat of sheer determination.

I had to fly into Cairo, connect to a flight to Luxor, arriving at midnight—and then spend a night in Luxor, with a six o'clock wake up call, in order to make the eight a.m. convoy departure—which I managed, just barely . . . but I did it.

As I sat in my private van, waiting for the convoy to depart, I asked myself: what better way to get ambushed by a terrorist hit squad than to assemble busloads of tourists and a few under-equipped police vans and head us out, like fast-moving sitting ducks, for a three-hour drive into the heartlands of the Sahara?

But that is Egypt. You learn to love it with all its idiosyncrasies and, to get those memorable moments, you learn to just leap—forgetting trying to make sense of any and all of it.

I committed to joining the convoy for this limited bird's eye view of Abydos, knowing I would need much more time and far more freedom than the short visit would ever allow me, but compelled, regardless, to get myself there—as if some ancient memory were calling me home. I know that I speak for so many people who have begun to hear the call back to special places in the world—places where they know, at some very deep level, they have walked before.

In the midst of the cacophony of vans and buses, police and submachine guns, I rode in quiet contemplation of what I would find in Abydos, gazing out the window, the Egyptian country-side whizzing by. We raced past so many beautiful faces of curious onlookers, peering back at us from their mud hut villages and fields: here the ox and plough; there the donkey, laden down with every kind of crop, burdened at the hand of man.

I felt stirred, knowing I was going far deeper into my Egyptian experience than I had before, flying below the radar of convention. It was an Egypt untouched by time, still moving at a pharaoh's pace while we, the outer world, raced past—ripping through the seamless fabric of people, place, and history.

What really compelled me to make this journey, I mused, and what secrets lay waiting to be revealed in Omm Sety's beloved Abydos?

At the end of the long drive, people scrambled from their respective buses, making the mad dash to the public restrooms, and then—just as frenetically—pushed their way noisily up the path-way to the hallowed halls of the majestic temple, framed against a cloudless morning sky.

Daunted by the crowd, I stepped back, preferring losing visiting time inside the temple to fighting my way through the groups and their nonstop-talking guides. As they stormed the path to the outer courtyard, I felt very little desire to actually enter the temple, for always my soul longs for silence and space when I take myself to sacred landscapes.

What could these people glean, I wondered, from such a visit—thrusting themselves noisily into this holy temple, rapists of the pure reverence and devotion of all those whose love and worship still hovered, in the ethers?

Right before you enter the temple courtyard gates, the footpath passes just to the side of a casual outdoor café, the Osiris Cafeteria, where the few foreigners living in Abydos spend their days in the bliss of life without time, without the noise of our harried world . . . without care.

I decided to stop there and enjoy a cup of spicy mint tea, while the hordes of tourists charged ahead, hoping they would clear out of the temple soon enough to provide me a chance at some private time inside, before we would all have to pile back into our buses and return to Luxor.

Sitting peacefully on a rickety old bamboo bench, I was able to detach myself from the scene: the flashing cameras, the irreverent laughter and the chatter of too many people attempting to do too much in too little time. I watched the throng of tourists disappear through the haze of Egyptian summer, the drone of their voices fading into the background, fading away as they passed through the portico of the temple.

I went within myself, celebrating the silence, the cool breezes, and the indolent morning sun. I cannot think of a time when I have experienced the pure essence of peace, washing over my soul, as deeply as I did then.

Gazing out upon the serene beauty of the Temple of Abydos, I was surprised at my own process: how I had lost all interest in the temple itself—the very reason I had come! For a while, I struggled with a sort of guilt feeling that I had not come so far to simply sit

49

in a café, but Abydos embraced me and those thoughts soon floated away. The village was every bit as important as the temple and there would be time—a right time—to enter.

"Maybe not this time," I mused, committing to following my instincts, and just enjoying the beauty of the sun's first rays over the village.

What magic awaits you when you first lay eyes upon this surreal scene: the temple etched against the blue sky, the mountains draping the desert beyond! Abydos is so special, so remote, you do really feel that you have turned back the hands of time. The energy is so pure and undisturbed you can almost hear the hymns and prayers of ancients, prayers to Isis and Osiris, calling you into their fields of worship.

Of all the grandeur and immensity of Egyptian architecture— the mammoth statues at Abu Simbel; the perfection of the Great Pyramids; the mighty Sphinx, effigy to Sirius—none has ever evoked within me such a deep sense of religious and spiritual reverence as the Temple of Sety I at Abydos.

It is about memory, I suppose, and all that floods back into your heart, as you hit the jackpot of your subconscious experience and the soul takes wing.

Knowing some higher force had pointed the way to Abydos, I opened myself, as I always have, to receiving whatever I was meant to find there. I sat in the stillness of that gentle morning light, waiting for the messengers to appear.

They always do. You need only listen, opening your heart and becoming absolutely receptive to what surrounds you.

To become a perfect magnet, calling those energies that are of the highest intention to come to you, is to know the pathway to supreme manifestation.

Snuggled in the warmth of this magical village, observer of its people and their ancient rhythms, I contemplated Omm Sety, whose incredible life story had clearly been the impetus that had drawn me here.

From the moment I read Jonathan Cott's book, I knew that I would one day come to Abydos to pick up the traces of Omm Sety, for I knew her essence would surely linger eternal in the hearts of the people who had known her, just as it would cling to the traces of spirits who still dwelled in Pharaoh Sety's temple to the gods.

To taste—if only for a moment—the magic of her passage from spirit, to form, and back to the otherworld, leaving a wave of wisdom and mystery in her wake, had been the true quest.

I knew that the temple, with all its beauty and history, was only a part of the mystery that had lured me to this sacred place.

Omm Sety herself had played the magic flute and I had followed, a willing captive, deaf to anything but the song of the enchantress.

One of the local boys, working as a waiter in the café, finally served the fragrant mint tea and I asked him if anyone there might be able to tell me about Omm Sety.

He understood enough English to be able to point me to the owner of the café, whom, he said, had known her and could tell me about her—and that is when I met Amir.

As he approached me—this gentle, elegant man—I knew at once that he was the true guardian of the temple grounds, the

51

spirit protector of this ancient world. Everything about him was priestly, noble, and yet completely unpretentious—an old soul still resonating to a much-loved place in realms of physical reality and earth time.

Wearing the traditional garb, the flowing galabieh, he exuded the light of a soul at peace in his world . . . and that world was Abydos. An imposing figure, he was at the same time innocent in the most delightful of ways—the picture of Upper Egypt and of a village that still retains the essence of the old ways.

Meeting him was really quite remarkable. It was a powerful old soul connection and I feel confident to say that we both knew it, intuitively, from the minute we set eyes on each other.

We didn't need words to define it. It simply **was.** The memory was buried, but its essence seemed to waft in the air around us. *See Frame 4.*

Without ever needing to speak the words, we knew that our ancient lifetime together had been one in the priesthood, which we had lived here, at Abydos. And here we were, together again.

In those precious first moments with Amir, we spoke almost exclusively of Omm Sety and her life in his village, as he generously shared what he could remember of her as a young boy. Eager to please, he took me to see the last house she had lived in before passing over. It was indeed a humble village mud hut, which she had continually co-inhabited, Amir recalled, with an endless number and assortment of grateful creatures.

He shared some pictures and a tattered copy of her classic work, *Abydos: Holy City of Ancient Egypt,*[3] reaching into his treas-

---

[3] Omm Sety and Hanny El Zeini, *Abydos: Holy City of Ancient Egypt* (Los Angeles: LL Co., 1981).

ure chest of memoirs in an attempt to bring her back to life for me, if only for just a moment, in those fleeting minutes before my departure.

Amir told me there were "many secrets" at Abydos awaiting my discovery. I knew this was an open invitation that I would definitely accept, somewhere just up ahead, on the pathway to the incredible revelations that have so defined my life and the pursuit of awakening.

But the convoy awaited, the buses belching poisonous fumes into the gentle breezes of Abydos—and no sooner had he sat down with me, it seemed, than it was time to leave. As hard as it was to tear myself away from Amir and without having much more than glanced at the entrance of what was certainly the holiest temple of Egypt, I was on my way just as quickly as I had arrived—knowing, at the very deepest levels of my soul, that I would spend many future days in the loving embrace of sacred Abydos.

As I tell this story some years later, I am proud and honored to say that Amir, the true guardian of Abydos temple, is a dear friend and brother and it is our remarkable destiny to be traveling the road to the mystery schools of Osiris together again, as we have no doubt done before: from the halls of Sety's temple, to the Osireion below... passing through the unknown realms in between.

Each of us brings back to the other a piece of an eternal story and, fitted together, the first reconnected images of a distant puzzle begin to take form in both our minds.

∿ 5
Abd'El Hakim Awyan
Last of the Indigenous
Wisdom Keepers of Khemit

Shortly after I returned from that visit to Egypt in 2001, I was swept up in the compelling experience of all that was emerging from my work as the voice of the Speakers of the Sirian High Council.

I have briefly described this connection with these light beings (which actually began in my childhood) as being activated back in 1996, after a truly incredible experience in the Julia Set crop circle in Wiltshire either rebundled some of my distracted DNA or burned some new neural highways in my brain. To this day I am not quite sure what happened there, but I do know that it was then that I began to receive the Sirian messages and that they have proven to be prophetically accurate, with regard to the unfolding of events at this time of Gaian evolution.

Moreover, they appear to be helping people face their fear of the unknown, while embracing the idea that we are evolving into a new consciousness, where the veil between our illusive, three-dimensional awareness and the higher "levels" is beginning to yield to the penetrating light of a new Age of Awakening—or, as the Sirians say, "a time of remembering."

During the ongoing process of connecting to this brilliant source of unconditional love and compassion, I have been shown how the Sirian star system is inextricably linked to the evolutionary process of life on our planet—and how the Sirian influence has been known to the human race from the earliest Atlantean civilizations, through the fabric of Egyptian history and into our contemporary times, the Age of Awakening, when so many people are remembering their Sirian roots. This has been elaborated in my previous books, which are dedicated works of love from the light beings of higher dimensions to the starseed of Earth.

More will come, since the Speakers are committed to assisting humankind make passage from this density as gentle and as conscious an experience as it can be.

However, now that I was opening new doors to mysteries that had begun to reveal themselves to me in Egypt, I had to understand how the Egypt-Sirius connection had contributed to the complexities of Egyptian magic and mysticism, as we are shown in the pantheon of their gods.

I longed to know the secrets of the pharaohs and I knew that these star beings could provide me more clues to lead me through my own mind and into the memories of ancient days. I became fascinated with the Egyptian imprint on my own consciousness, at the personal level, and upon human experience as a whole.

I couldn't go any further into my Egyptian initiations without understanding the celestial dynamics of the Sirian system and their interaction with our central sun, Ra, articulated in this passage from my book *The Starseed Dialogues:*

Ours is a complex stellar family: a multidimensional trinity of parallel universes in which our three stars currently hold resonance.

As such, the Sirian Sisterhood "imprints" the Cosmos with the vibratory signature of a nonlinear fractal design, perpetually co-creating the multidimensional Universe in a breathtaking array of stellar and planetary harmonics and cosmometric proportions.

You can understand why we are so attuned to the concept of triangulation, the dynamic interrelationships of aspects that form the numerical imprint of three . . . and why it is so very basic to the knowledge we attempt to share with you as we communicate through our instrument, the channel who brings our message to you.

It is the combined consciousness of our three stellar deities that defines the One and, as such, the evolutionary progression of each is defined by the All—the Sisterhood of Three.

If we may use the metaphor of the combined notes of a symphony, the three sister stars would be best described as a musical chord of three harmonious notes on the diatonic scale, but each sounding from a different octave.

We ask you to imagine how each is a reflection of the other and how the stellar framework forms a multidimensional merkaba of light, sound, and soul. That music rings eternal through the dimensions, uniting all the consciousness units of this celestial sphere— a bass chord in the music of infinity.

Together as One (for we are One, despite our differences), all conscious beings of the realm form the chorus, creating our overlying melody, as the orchestra plays the song of Creation under the superb direction of Prime Creator . . . the Grand Maestro. . . .

Let us elaborate . . . the stellar composition of Sirius and the planets of each stellar deity, with the specifics of each:

Sothis (Sirius A) *shines in your three-dimensional holographic galaxy as the brightest light in your northern hemisphere—far more* *luminous than your own star, Ra, and the fifth closest star (in linear terms) to yours.*

It currently holds vibration on the third dimension, gracing your celestial canopy with the brilliant light that has long inspired civilizations of Homo sapiens, *since the time of your inception, as it has others—on the sister planets of your solar system—comprising the physical, spiritual, and mental bodies of Ra.*

It was once the gravitational anchor of a number of planetary bodies similar to your Earth, upon which liquid water was available in abundance to all life forms and climates were warm and steamy—much like those of your equatorial zones.

Extremely dense atmospheres shielded the inner planets of Sothis from the scorching ultraviolet rays and gases, allowing untold species of aquatic life as well as incredibly complex fauna to flourish on those planetary surfaces: from the minutiae of single cell amoebae, to the complexity of the most exquisite vertebrates—many of which exist on Earth as well.

Countless species mirroring biological earth life (those with which you are familiar and endless others, still unidentified) exist on other planets, particularly within the family of planetary bodies that comprise your own solar system.

The organization of subatomic particles always follows the intelligent design of Creation and these cosmometric patterns appear throughout all time, space, and dimension.

Many are the creatures of your oceans—from the deep, dark abyss of the deepest seas to sun-laced shallow waters—that also procreate in the vast oceans across the Cosmos of Soul.

Although you have studied and observed countless species of your oceans, your marine biologists have yet to understand, in its entirety, the complexity of form and interdependency within the seas. They have not yet understood the interplay between the layers of light and dark, treble and bass, absorption and refraction and the weaving of consciousness from sea floor to surface and back again.

Certain species of the seas are so remote in your most inaccessible environments that you have yet to even imagine their existence— and yet they are there, as they are elsewhere, in the Cosmos.

As close as your deepest oceans, then, life exists where you have been taught to believe it cannot—as it does not fit into the boundaries of what science has allowed (until now) as "probable environments" in which biological life can flourish.

Despite the various belief systems, speculation, and hypotheses of your more conservative scientific voices, we assure you that life (as it occurs on Earth) abounds, in varied and similar forms, at several stopping points in your solar realm . . . and beyond.

Life is the driving force of the universe of matter. It is the essential nature of the Universe! All is thought; all is motion; all is manifestation. Earth, which in many ways you still perceive as the center of your universe, is but a drop in the greatest ocean—a second in the infinity of timeless beauty.

As for Sirius A, our three-dimensional star: we do confirm to you that, at this point on the space-time continuum, there is no intelligent (as you understand it) biological life in its greater stellar body.

What does exist there is more easily described as the "subatomic data base" of previous biological life forms—awaiting the proper coordinates on that time line to reactivate.

Satais (Sirius B) *was once the giant of the triangulation of stars that comprise the Sirian family of solar deities. Throughout its duration in the 3D realm, it was the leviathan of the solar trinity as it* *was the life-bearer of twelve planetary satellites that have all ascended to the higher dimensions.*

It currently holds frequency on the sixth dimension, and the light bodies of those planets that orbited Satais continue to hold the celestial coordinates—the harmonics—which reflect the dynamic makeup of that system.

Not all ascended Sirians reside here with us in the sixth dimension, but we, Sirians of the High Council, come to you from this light frequency. Some have gone on to higher realms; some have retrograded to lower densities to work with other life forms, focusing consciousness to reach attunement there—in very much the same way as we reach you, via our dedicated instrument, Trydjya.

What is seen orbiting Sothis in your three-dimensional telescopic fields is the skeletal form of that stellar being, left behind as a marker of what once was a part of your density. It ascended long ago into light body, as have the planets and living beings that resided there.

Of the many beings who have progressed with Satais, it is those of us in this dimension (the sixth) who are directly concerned with earth affairs, for reasons that have been amply explained to you in prior works ... but we wish to reemphasize that there are other light beings from the Satais imprint, who are bringing their love and wisdom to the many other worlds in need of assistance, at this phase of Ra's imminent ascension.

They are heart-centered, loving participants in the spiral stream upon which we all contribute enormous energy and experience, as it is the mission of all light beings to assist others, further down the spiral, in their journey back to Source.

You have this to look forward to in ways you may still find difficult to imagine ... perhaps not until you reach the next level of awareness, when you are truly living in unconditional love for all the people, places, beings, and life forms—loving even the darkest ones, whom you know will eventually return to Source, just like you.

***Anu (Sirius C)** is the third of our complex stellar interface. In the three-dimensional phase of its development, it was the source of life for five primary planetary bodies and a significant quantity of lifeless (in biological terms) formations, which most closely resemble that which you have identified as the "asteroid" in your own system.*

It passed to the fourth dimension and still resonates to the consciousness of that density, determined by the evolutionary progress of that Solar Logos and the celestial deities of her physical being.

As you have gleaned from our texts, The Sirian Revelations, *Nebiru was one planet of Anu that has remained in the 3D realm. Of the intelligent life forms of the other four, there have been species that have retrograded into the earth biosphere (at different points in your planet's evolution) to assist and serve the human race.*

Amongst these were the predecessors of the Dolphin Beings— made immortal through the teachings of the Ancient Dogon peoples of the land mass you know as Africa.

—The Starseed Dialogues[4]

The question of extraterrestrial involvement in earth affairs is one that will be heatedly debated by skeptics and believers right up until that one day when we have global contact—a day that is nearly upon us. Even then, when aliens from other worlds stand boldly before us, finally revealed, the die-hard materialists will most likely deny what they see. Such events would be outside their experience, just as the implications of the arrival of European ships were initially lost on the Native Americans.

---

[4]Patricia Cori, *The Starseed Dialogues* (Berkeley, CA: North Atlantic Books, 2009).

Communication of the extra-dimensional sort seems to solicit even greater resistance than the idea of intelligent life of the three-dimensional variety and that is understandable. Many are the self-declared "channels," myself included, coming forth with messages from the "beyond." It can be a swamp of conflicting ideas—some preposterous, others more feasible—that the reader needs to wade through. Never has the need for discernment been greater.

I do believe that it is important that people weigh the information for what it is, rather than fixating on where it comes from. Otherwise, the nature of the rational mind to focus on the doubt, rather than the possibility, negates any wisdom that can be gleaned from the message itself.

In the meantime, however, the idea that beings from other realms and dimensions might have been directly involved with ancient societies of our Earth is, for the most part, still dismissed as "fantasy" by the conventional historians and archeologists. Nowhere, it seems, is this more true than in Egypt, where the classicists still cling to the banal explanations we have heard recounted, over and over again: the probable time lines of the greatest civilizations of pre-history; the purpose of the monuments that still remain; the meanings of the glyphs and magnificent sculptures they left behind.

Fortunately, there are pioneers, such as noted authors Murry Hope and Robert Temple, tuned in to the Sirian pulse, who have created brilliant and academic works, in which their study of the Dogon tribes of Africa and of other record keepers provide us with rather astounding proofs of Sirian intervention on Earth. Their books are treasure chests of possible realities from which one can only deduce that the Sirian imprint lies throughout

Egyptian myth and magic . . . and well before recorded history, the time of the forty-two tribes of Africa, which, united, comprised the Land of Khemit.

Fortunately, indeed, there is Hakim. *See Frame 5.*

The last of the Khemitian wisdom keepers, Abd'El Hakim Awyan resides in the village of Nazlet El Samman in Giza, just in front of the Great Sphinx and the pyramids. Many a sunny day have I spent with him, sitting on his balcony, from where the Great Pyramid frames the background of photos of our blessed times together.

Meeting Hakim is truly the opening of a door upon the no-time, where truth lies before the seeker, in all its simplicity and innocence. I, and others who have had the honor and the great gift of knowing and learning from him, know him as a true Master, a walking reservoir of information that speaks to his deeper knowledge of Egyptian and pre-Egyptian history—the wisdom of people and civilizations that outdate the pharaonic era by tens of thousands of years.

I have been blessed to spend much time with him, drinking in what I can of his brilliance and his diligent memory of the oral tradition of those who came before the great civilizations of recorded Egyptian history.

I believe he holds the keys to unlocking the secrets of Egypt's unfathomable past. Moreover, he is a model of the potential within us all, a true Renaissance man, and just knowing him is a gift beyond measure.

Hakim is no mere raconteur of ancient lore and myth, although he has been trained in the oral tradition by Elders of his tribe. He was the one chosen, so long ago, to take his rightful place as the Khemitian wisdom keeper of this, the Age of Awakening.

I understand he is also a graduate of Cairo University, holding dual degrees in Egyptology and in archeology, and has done graduate work abroad. His knowledge and wisdom are solid, equally formed of logic and intuition—a beautiful balance of the harmonized male/female mind.

At the core of his teachings is the understanding that a highly sophisticated civilization, the Khemit, existed in Africa well before the time line of recorded history and that, contrary to the predominant mindset, the Golden Age in the land of the Sahara dates back tens of thousands of years before the record would have us believe.

Hakim is not particularly fond of the Atlantis hypothesis, which is based upon the theory that prehistoric people of a high culture on Earth—the Great Atlanteans—eventually migrated to Africa, after the cataclysm described in so many traditions as the Great Flood of 10,800 BC, to establish the high civilization of early Egypt.

Some believe it was these very immigrants, priests and priestesses of that mysterious civilization, who were the icons that became the immortalized gods of the first pharaonic kingdoms, and that the revered gods Osiris and Isis were actually human beings—great rulers from the Atlantean Kingdom.

On the touchy subject of Atlantis, one that has evoked many a heated discussion between us, Hakim does concede that it could well have existed, contemporarily, alongside the extended civilization of the Khemitians and that it may well be that his ancestors exchanged their knowledge and wisdom with Atlantean explorers, even merchants, reaching the shores of the Black Land of Egypt.

That the people of pre-dynastic Egypt were mere shepherds

and barbarians, however, he refuses unequivocally, with a vengeance, in honor of his ancestors.

According to Hakim, there is no question that the Creator God, Ptah, descended from the star system of Sirius. From the complexities of Egyptian mythology, and the many different systems and epochs of gods in evolution, comes a common belief that Ptah, as the Father of all Creation, called the world into existence by "speaking it" into being.

This same description of Creation is recounted in the later Judeo-Christian texts. The Gospel of John describes how "In the beginning was the Word."

The word is "intended" sound; that sound is focused vibration; the vibration is energy being brought to manifestation.

Egyptian art depicts Ptah as a mummified man, wearing a blue skullcap, holding the *ankh* (symbol of eternal life), the *djed* (symbol of stability), and the *was* rod (symbol of power).

From the onset, says Hakim, the Creator God, Ptah, must be recognized as "the one who popped in from the blue, through the waters, from the stars." According to the Khemitian tradition, this is why Ptah is always depicted in blue skin tones (although some would argue that they are green), as I would later see so clearly in the temple at Abydos—and why he is always depicted wearing a bright blue cap, symbol of the blue-white star—Sirius.

Stephen Mehler, perhaps the closest person to Hakim (outside of his family), and author of the most complete book of Hakim's teachings, *The Land of Osiris,* remained as stupefied as I was when he heard this information for the first time. He tells of how he was visiting the museum with Hakim, and how his "jaw hit the floor" at the realization that the Khemitians were quite possibly saying that Ptah was from the Sirian star system.

Later, Stephen would confirm that the ancient Khemitians were obsessed with Sirius and that their term for Sirius was *Sa-Ptah*, which translated as the "birthplace of Ptah."

I was no less astonished than he when Hakim shared this important piece of the Sirio-Egyptian puzzle with me directly: not so much so by the content of the information, but by the fact that it was confirming what I had absorbed and integrated from the Sirian Speakers in my earlier works.

Yet it was so obvious, really. There was evidence here: the depiction of the deity with his bright blue cap, the blue hue of his skin, and the memory of the Khemitian Elders, told through their wisdom keeper, Hakim. No other Egyptian god bears these traits. The Creator God, Ptah, was the one who "popped in" to this dimension, through the vibrational frequencies of the waters, reflecting the bluish hues of the brightest star in the heavens.

He was the Great Sirian Emissary of Ancient Days.

There are very significant clues here, indications of the origins of humanity, tying together the myths and oral traditions of many cultures and confirming the voice of the Sirian Speakers that forever echoes the same message in my head.

In Mehler's excellent work, he and Hakim elaborate upon the depiction of Ptah, whom Hakim asks Stephen to identify by race. He concludes that Ptah, with his Asian eyes, Caucasian nose, and Negroid lips, appears to be a representation of "many races, as the father or progenitor race of Sirius." According to Stephen Mehler, Hakim was "clearly indicating the Khemitian indigenous tradition for Sirius as a 'starseed' hypothesis for human origins."

This fits like a glove with the teachings of *The Sirian Revelations,* in which the Speakers describe the Sirian's Great Experiment, when beings from that star system seeded the Earth with four primary racial archetypes, so that the evolved species of *Homo sapiens* would endure and prosper.

According to the material, Earth was the chosen "Garden of Eden" in which to birth a Golden Race of light beings who were intended as the guardians of the material universe, and it was the involvement of Sirian Elders that actually birthed us through interspecies, multidimensional genetic engineering, not unlike the experiments our scientists are performing (devoid of the love and compassion of our ancestors) on various animal species today.

It is not that far-fetched anymore, now, is it?

The selection of different species, as represented, according to Hakim, in the facial characteristics depicted in the renderings of Ptah, was deemed necessary for the longevity of our species, as described in the teachings of the High Council:

Intensive studies were made of the existing environments of Earth—the distinctive plant and animal kingdoms—and detailed investigations were conducted into how bio-diversity resulted as a reflection of various geophysical and climatic variables. It was discerned that such diversity would provide ideal conditions for the seeding of extraterrestrial species, as their original environments could, in many ways, be replicated in the ecosystems of Earth. And, oh, the bountiful waters! No other planet offered such an abundance of the life-bearing element—the essential resource for life throughout the Universe.

The engineers of the Great Experiment knew that if the weakening of the species' genetic pool were to be avoided, a balance of distinctly diverse genetic codes would have to be introduced into the DNA matrix, so that interbreeding would strengthen the race, rather than weaken it, as is so often the case in other worlds and isolated species. Earth offered the ecological diversity and the resources needed to successfully introduce the variant genetic codes and provide for their incubation.

Here lie the true origins of the four master races on Earth ... so very unique in their make-up, while of a common "galactic" nature and intent.

Unexplained in your archeological and missing-link evolutionist theories is the isolated emergence upon your planet of four distinct seed races. These, we can tell you, are archetypes of master races, whose fundamental genetic material formed the primary "substance" of your race, while the vibrational patterns and sequencing of extra-dimensional beings (those of the higher realms) were woven into the intricate light codes of your incredible twelve-stranded DNA.

The genetic material of these four primary races was united in the blueprint of the species of Homo sapiens. *While combining the DNA of the four races into one matrix, the master geneticists varied the strains so that the predominant genetic material resulting from a given planetary or stellar frequency would be seeded in those specific Gaian climates that most closely resembled the original environment, which they were convinced would best facilitate the successful development of the prototype. This, we reiterate, was intended to strengthen your genetic pool, for the eventual interbreeding of* Homo sapiens *would, in this way, ensure your survival.*

—No More Secrets, No More Lies[5]

---

[5]Patricia Cori, *No More Secrets, No More Lies* (Berkeley, CA: North Atlantic Books, 2008).

To realize that we come from the stars, or rather, to remember our starseed origins, is most likely the one most significant discovery of our individual and collective experience as human beings on this rapidly evolving planet. Slowly but surely, we are putting those pieces back together, activating the dormant within us and reassembling the scattered bits of our DNA, of which ninety percent has forever been declared "junk" within us. I believe that these pieces of our incredible genetic history are the keys to discovering a greater ancestry, our galactic family, and that now is the exciting time in which we are reassembling that information . . . regaining the lost memories.

Even the most die-hard rationalists are slowly moving toward a new paradigm—one that embraces the possibility that we truly are seed of other star systems. But is it "new," or are we simply retrieving the knowledge of the ancients, who appear to have had assistance (at many important locations and in infinite time frames on this planet) from beyond? The clues are everywhere, all across this globe, where humankind has left clues of interaction with other worlds, but nowhere, I find, is the Sirian connection as clearly mapped out for us as it is in Egypt.

To learn how the Egyptians and their great ancestors of Atlantean times, the Khemitians, idolized the Sirian light beings who walked upon this Earth in the ancient days has everything to do with our history, our evolution, and our imminent awakening from the age of the "hidden," which Hakim defines as the era of *Amen,* into the Age of *Khepre,* the light of Dawn.

Is it any wonder that the pharaohs, enlightened to the knowledge of their true origins, lived to return to the stars—that they might dwell as their Sirian gods—a message I had heard, echoing like ripples of thought upon the winds of time, through the temple halls at Deir el-Bahri?

∾ 6

Initiation by Fire

It was becoming more and more difficult to devote myself to my busy life in Rome with Egypt calling me, taunting, luring me back. Something indefinable had been stirred within me and my thoughts mirrored how my spirit longed to be there, grounded in the sands of the Sahara in one minute ... walking through portals in the next.

There was one particularly irrational moment, just months after my return to Rome, when I was on the way to the bank and found myself, instead, standing, rather hypnotically, at the entrance of the EgyptAir office. Impulsively, I ended up buying myself a round-trip ticket with funds that were supposed to be going into my account for the monthly bills (adult mind)—not for journeys into the unknown (the child speaking!).

By then, I had enriched my first impressions of Egypt with extensive reading, which provided a basic understanding of the history and the perplexing myths of the ancients. I was introduced to the complex family of Egyptian gods (the neteru), who inspired pharaohs and peasants from the beginning of the High Culture of the earliest civilizations to the later societies and who still beguile and inspire contemporary seekers: adventurers ... such as me.

Having been guided by Sekhmet through the underworld in that transformational initiation in the subterranean chamber of the Great Pyramid, I wanted to learn all I could about this powerful goddess of the fiery soul, activator of the power chakra—that spinning energy vortex at the solar plexus.

The guard who had stood at the tomb in my past life terror play also came to life from the pages of a book, just exactly as I had seen him in those visions: Ra, who the ancients believed died at the end of each day and sailed through the underworld through the night . . . to be reborn the day after.

I was particularly fascinated with Hathor, the deity who reigns over the "temple within the temple" of Hatshepsut—such an obvious depiction of an alien being, with her piercing human eyes and strange, cow-like ears. I would be fascinated to learn, later on, that she was believed to be the alter ego of Sekhmet, Isis in "changeling" form.

And what of Osiris, Lord of the Underworld . . . Isis, his consort . . . had they really lived, as recounted by Herodotus, the fifth-century Greek sage, as human beings among the ancients, exiles from another, contemporaneous civilization—perhaps Atlantis? What untold secrets still lay hidden in the myths of the earliest gods?

I had to connect with these archetypes in a deeper, more meaningful way and I knew that no amount of research would ever provide me more than theory, drawn from endless interpretations of historians, archeologists, and the range of Egyptologists who have done so much to decipher the records. I needed more. I would have to immerse myself in their energies completely, to get to the source, unfettered.

If you can attune to it—if you can hear the music of ancient song, you can relive the experience of all that has passed before. If you can reach resonance with a given frequency, you can retrieve the conscious thought that defines that frequency, just as you can recognize how it will play out on the horizons of new dawns over the realms of conscious awareness.

I left for Egypt again, abandoning my ever-patient partner, Franco, and my dogs, home, and job, compelled by a force I still did not understand, but following the lead of whatever or whomever was driving me to turn the mystical pages of unwritten history.

Once again, I booked myself straight through to Luxor, avoiding the madness of Cairo completely, as my intention was to return to the mysterious Temple of Hatshepsut near the Valley of the Kings, where I knew much more awaited my discovery.

First, though, I would dedicate myself to exploring the renowned Karnak Temple at Luxor, ancient Thebes, the most elaborate temple complex of all Egypt. It is a city in itself, filled with every imaginable trace of worship to gods and kings ... with its pillars and statues that seem to pierce the sky ... and still today I have only scratched the surface of all that awaits the seeker in my explorations there. *See Frame 6.*

I always get sidetracked.

At this temple site is found a relatively well hidden, nondescript little building, which houses a sanctuary to the Creator God, Ptah, and his consort, the lion goddess, Sekhmet. It is she who was my captain on the great ship upon which I had sailed, years (and probably many lifetimes) earlier from the pit of the Great Pyramid, across the twelve gates of the underworld.

If you do not know where to look for this remarkable treasure, you will most likely never run across it, as it lies off a sandy pathway to the side of the main temple complex, and there are no indications of its whereabouts inside the grounds, where mainstream tourist activity is focused.

The temple of Ptah and Sekhmet does appear, quite often, on special "sacred journey" programs offering metaphysical tours of Egypt, however, because it is so crucial to the initiatory experience.

We metaphysicians seem to know the incredible energy and mystery it holds.

It is as if only those with the highest intentions are meant to enter that incredibly powerful space and so, to this day, it remains relatively undisturbed by the flashing cameras, noise, and crowds of tourists who have more than enough to take in from the archeological wonders of Karnak's imposing grounds.

Recalling Hakim's description of Ptah as "the one who popped in from the blue, through the waters, from the stars," and feeling the familiar vibrations that I have known in my channeling sessions with the Sirian High Council, I instantly realized, entering this sanctuary for the first time, that here I was in a temple of Sirian influence and that both Ptah and his consort, Sekhmet, had been joined here, as guardians of the gateways to my resonant star system, Sirius.

Ptah

Unfortunately, the effigy of Ptah today is headless, no doubt dismembered by some irreverent looter who probably sold the sculptured head to a private collector or museum, many moons ago.

After meditating in front of the statue of Ptah for the first time, I opened my eyes and was startled to see a face actually staring back at me. The head of the statue appeared to still be there, just barely holding on to the third dimension—but there nonetheless, like the proverbial severed limb, which holds its imprint in the ethers, although it is no longer a part of the living organism and no longer exists in the physical realm.

Years and many fellow journeyers later, I have yet to have anyone else report having had this experience and yet every time I enter his temple, the head of Ptah is visible to me; his face looks back at me: those deep, Sirian eyes look back.

Curious that there is no record of this phenomenon, I have photographed the statue and played with some of the filters of the digital tools now available to us to change the lighting of the shot—but the image itself has not been doctored in any way. *See Frames 7 and 8.*

You will see that the etheric imprint of the head appears, even in the photo, offering somewhat of a "validating experience" to the case for the etheric presence of the Creator God, manifest in a three-dimensional framework.

Ptah's damaged icon lies directly at the entrance, in the first chamber of the temple, while Sekhmet stands in a secondary chamber, ruling over her own private space, to the right of Ptah.

Having experienced the lion goddess, Sekhmet, psychically, as a humble initiate in the pyramid, I was amazed to rediscover her, just as she had appeared to me then, as a powerful feline effigy there at Karnak, in her Theban sanctuary. I was overwhelmed to have received such precise validation that this majestic being, who had appeared to me in that powerful vision, had actually existed in Egyptian history, and I was filled with gratitude at having been given the

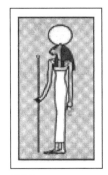

Sekhmet

opportunity to experience that, undisturbed and alone, at that pivotal moment in my journey.

To gaze upon her majestic form and to feel such waves of energy—the pure consciousness of spirit made manifest through the dense matter of stone—was an experience that I will carry with me for the rest of my days.

Carved from a huge block of black basalt, the mighty lioness reigns over that small, silent room in relative darkness—her only light a mere wisp of sun that shines, from a slit in the ceiling, into her peering, all-knowing black eyes. *See Frame 9.*

Whoever built this space, I believe, intended that the two gods would both remain there through eternity and that fiery Sekhmet would forever stand somehow "contained" by the space itself, as if exposing her to any more than just that hint of the sun's light might unleash some unknowable, dangerous quantum of her explosive essence upon the world.

On the many occasions when I conduct ceremonies at the Temple of Sekhmet, she activates at the moment she becomes aware of her worshippers returning (for we do believe we have been there before) into the darkness of that space, where we come to celebrate her as the Protector—the Great Mother. Almost all who enter into her lonely, dark cell can feel the fire of indescribable force and beauty, as they experience the consciousness—the vital life force—of what the uninitiated see only as cold, black stone.

Nothing you can read or imagine prepares you for the intensity of this encounter with this Sirian lioness, Sekhmet. As a shamanic facilitator to those who journey with me, I have been witness to incredible displays of energy pouring from the statue and have always come away with a sense of respectful awe and an even more profound connection with the force of her power.

Many are the initiates who will testify to their own life-changing encounters with this goddess of fire.

Like her headless partner, Ptah, the divine spirit of Sekhmet lives eternally through her ancient effigy and, activated, she flashes that essence at you, gazing deeply into your soul, imprinting your very DNA, if only you will dare to enter and ask to unlock the secrets she holds in that sacred space.

She speaks through those eyes, touching you ... reaching you at the deepest levels of your conscious awareness, and then moves into the subconscious to stoke the fire that burns within.

It is a humbling experience to stand before Sekhmet, I assure you. You can feel the immense power, just as you can hear her silent roar echoing through the ethers ... and you can most definitely sense the potential for the fire of her spirit to burn right through you.

She is Initiation by Fire.

There is a dual nature to this statue, which reflects the two-fold personality of the goddess. On the one hand, you observe the tame, docile lioness, adorned by the moon disk—that is what most people report seeing when they come out of the chamber. This is her lunar, reflective self.

Sekhmet Statue

On the other hand, you are confronted with a mighty, almost alien creature, as she mutates in and out of her three-dimensional persona. Here the disk appears as a disproportionate skull and the ears of the lioness, now flaming eyes, flicker in the light overhead. This is the fiery, solar aspect, untamed and explosive.

77

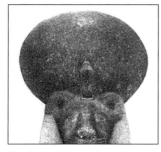

Another View of Sekhmet

This is the Sekhmet that I always see.

That the mighty statue is positioned here, in this dark chamber, in such a way, with the small opening shooting light into her eyes, is true testimony to the Egyptians' understanding of the dual nature of the reality in which we find ourselves, as residents of the third dimension ... particularly now, when we are bouncing about in the extreme polarity of our earthly revolution.

Shrouded in near total darkness, mighty Sekhmet stands eternal. She is a teacher of the higher wisdom, revealing to us how the gods embody the resolution of that polarity: dark and light, evil and goodness, fear and love exalted.

Ptah, no less mighty, shows us how consciousness and the manifestation of focused intent permeate all the layers of reality. Let this be testimony, I tell myself, that all that exists remains forever imprinted in the ethers, recorded in the Akashic Record: the All That Is, That Ever Was, and That Always Will Be.

The Sirian gods at Karnak are "alive," their essence encapsulated in the molecular structure of their stony "incarnations." Their carved effigies are imprinted with the consciousness of countless worshippers, from so many thousands of years before us, to this very day. They are alive with the hope and fear and devotion of pharaohs and the priests of Thebes and they scintillate with the energies and intentions of those who have knelt before them, perhaps from the very beginning of time.

They teach us to go beyond the veil of illusion, where everything is possible, daring us to see past the constraints of our limited three-dimensional experience, where we recognize that everything that exists is alive and that all life is One. We are reminded, in their mighty presence, how all that is represented in the theater of the physical universe is energy and that energy is pure consciousness.

Everything is.

Everything has been.

Everything remains.

Like the kaleidoscope, forms change to create new illusions ...but the essence of form is everlasting.

To bring to full awareness the experience of interacting with live deities through the density of their camouflage of dense stone is truly to reach a milestone on the journey of initiation into the alchemy of the spiritual experience, through which we transform the "lead" of ignorance into the "gold" of enlightened mind.

The consciousness of even one brain cell contains the memory of all existence, as does one molecule of any mineral matrix. We link conscious units of one form, the human mind, to another, the mineral kingdom, and the exchange between "consciousness streams" imprints both, to be stored and remembered in the Akashic Record.

The experience is life-altering and eternal.

Interestingly, of the many people I have had the pleasure to guide to Egypt through my SoulQuest™ mystical journeys, almost all have declared that moment with Sekhmet, when they stand or kneel before her alone in the chapel, as the most powerful of all their Egyptian experiences: more powerful than lying in the granite "sarcophagus" inside the King's Chamber in the

Great Pyramid . . . even more incredible, for some, than entering into the mighty arms of the Great Sphinx.

That is the awesome power of Sekhmet and she let us have a taste of it, in all its transformational glory, during one of my annual programs to Egypt, back in 2005.

That year, we spent some utterly breathtaking moments in Cairo, where I arranged private entrance for our group into the Great Pyramid. After two indescribable hours inside the greatest "time machine" of the world, the Great Pyramid, we accessed the forbidden area in front of the Sphinx, just outside of her paws . . . the greatest Sirian portal on this Earth. *See Frame 10.*

Following these truly privileged, remarkable moments at Giza, we left for Luxor, to explore the sites of Upper Egypt, where temples along the Nile correspond to chakra vortices of the human body.

I bring people there to tune in to the harmonic frequencies that are encoded in the sacred sites and to activate those chakric energy wheels within (themselves mere notes on the keyboard of our musical bio-systems), as part of a journey of alignment, DNA activation, and initiation into the alchemical secrets of Egyptian mysticism.

It is a deeply moving, sometimes overwhelming epiphany for all who make the pilgrimage.

I brought my group first to Karnak Temple, specifically to the sacred chapels of Ptah and Sekhmet, as part of the process of Initiation by Fire with the Sirian goddess: activation of the power chakra.

As always, I approached the temple with reverence and respect. I entered ahead of them, laying my humility and respect before the goddess Sekhmet, like a garland of love, asking her to acknowledge the presence of devoted worshippers who had come to honor her and to receive her blessings.

I asked for permission to "turn the key"; the key, she showed me, was the ankh she holds in her right hand. I had only to understand how to receive it, from her mighty interdimensional energy fields to my eager psychic hands. *See Frame 11.*

As I reached out to the great goddess of fire, an unfamiliar utterance sounded through my mind and I spoke it, out loud.

Almost immediately, I could feel the statue activate, the room electrified by the consciousness that was woven into that space. Permission was granted for me to "accompany the seekers" one by one, so that each could know the privacy of that moment of reverence—the appointed hour that, for many, may very well have been thousands of years in the waiting.

I stood at the entry to the chamber, welcoming each into the small space, privileged to observe those first encounters, when awakening souls bring the memory of Sekhmet to the foreground of their experience. They are stripped of ego and expectation, knowing the greatness of something so powerful it defies description, and (if they are truly blessed) they experience the magnificence of humility, abandoning all other acquired knowledge to be in the moment: receptive and innocent and, above all, humble.

Some were instantly brought to tears, others fell to their knees, yet others were moved to deeper, unexplored emotions. With each, I stood at the back of the room, holding the space. I was so privileged to share and assist in the awesome process of these unsuspecting seekers, who had no idea of just what awesome force awaited them there, in the lair of the great lioness.

It was an honor to be part of their experience, a blessing that plays the heartstrings and fills my soul with gratitude.

Of these fifty individuals, only one person felt nothing—nothing at all. She entered, looked around the room, clearly unimpressed, walked right up to the statue, and slammed her hand over the face of Sekhmet with such derision that it broke the magic of what had been created up to that moment—magic for all who had entered before her.

She looked back at me as if to say, "So what's the big deal?" and reached for her camera.

I could actually see the energy shift. The room became unbearably hot, the soft light in Sekhmet's eyes turned to fire, and a **cold** shiver ran from my neck all the way down to my feet.

"You desecrate my temple?" Sekhmet roared through the ethers, her eyes glaring down upon the woman like burning hot coals. It was an immense, overwhelming energy, a force so powerful it literally threw me crashing up against the wall behind me, as her rage permeated the space.

My assistant, Beata, who was in the Ptah chamber at the time, said she saw my body actually lift off the ground, before I went smashing into the back wall of Sekhmet's enclosure.

It was an experience of such magnitude that neither I, nor any others in the group, who felt the huge wave of energy roll through them, will ever forget it.

At that precise moment, the magic ended—like a clock that suddenly stops ticking. Trouble began to brew outside and even from inside the chamber I could hear a heated exchange of loud male voices, shouting at each other in Arabic. It was totally disruptive and destroyed what was left of the wonder and love we had felt during our ceremony, which ended, but had not been completed, there and then.

I felt called to intervene, to calm the waters, but I knew I could not leave Sekhmet until this violation had been healed and the balance—the love—had been restored to her sacred space.

My second assistant, Laura, came forward from outside and agitatedly whispered to me that there was a problem outside.

The problem, I told her, was greater **inside,** with Sekhmet, and I told her to tell Ahmed, our tour guide, to "handle it." Whatever was erupting from the fires of Sekhmet's soul, it was his job to manage the outer, denser manifestation, while I worked to suppress and extinguish the burning flames of subtler realms.

Everything changed from that moment.

The time of worship was over—I knew that the events unfolding outside were a reflection of Sekhmet manifesting her rage. I brought the ceremony to a halt and headed over to the men where "trouble" was fast turning into "danger."

Ahmed called me aside to describe what had taken place while I was inside the temple. Apparently, another guide had come to the temple with his group and he was furious that we were blocking his people from going inside, since we had no permit for a private visit.

Trying to stall for time so that I could complete the ritual, Laura had tried to reason with the man that we were well near finishing and asked him to allow us another thirty minutes to get all the group through, but he ranted about his rights—demanding that our guide either hand over the special permit required for group visits or that we get out immediately.

When Ahmed could not produce the document, but still adamantly refused to interrupt the ceremony, the guide stormed off to find the tourist police and report him.

Ahmed worriedly whispered to me that, having facilitated a group to conduct a ceremony without permission, he would be in real trouble if the police came and that he could even possibly be arrested.

He was wild, his eyes full of fear.

With the guide soon to return with the tourist police, Ahmed had come up with an "offensive defense" by enlisting Laura in a deceptive counterattack, whereby she was to declare that the guide of the other group had touched her in "an inappropriate manner." The idea was to discredit the man to the point that he would drop his charge against Ahmed and, in so doing, defuse the attack against him—but it was a lie.

He had not touched her improperly. This man stood tall in his truth, and Laura (coerced into playing the part to save Ahmed's skin) and Ahmed did not—plain and simple.

Fifty people, having just been initiated into the Egyptian mysteries, stood, mystified, and watched as the drama played out: Laura, the wounded "victim" of the offense; the guide, staunchly fighting for his honor; Ahmed, acting out his part; the tourist policeman. Like a scene from a Fellini movie, all the players acted their roles in the human drama as I watched, recognizing how the true initiation—Sekhmet taking us through the flames of purification—was unfolding for us all.

Knowing I had to get the group away from the disturbance in order not to destroy what had been experienced in our magnificent ceremony with Sekhmet, I asked the policeman's permission to allow the group to return to our ship (which was set to sail within one hour) and leave the interested parties with him. He looked at the group and agreed, knowing there was not much of a choice but to let the rest of the group go.

Leaving Laura and Ahmed to deal with the police, I guided the group back to the bus and we drove off to quieter space, our cruise ship—where people could have the time to integrate what had been given to them in their time with Sekhmet.

Once back at the ship, I found the agitated tour company representative in heated discussion via cell phone with Ahmed. The situation by now was completely out of hand. The outraged guide was pressing charges against Ahmed, and the police were indeed threatening to arrest him. The tourist police had taken all of them to the Police Station: the guide, Laura, Ahmed, and two of my group, whom the agent singled out as "witnesses." They had been asked to come and report their observations of what had happened to the Chief of Police, although I was pretty sure it was more about their being the most attractive women in the group.

I reflected on how the lack of compassion and respect had manifested into such ugliness, as I was whisked off the ship and taken to the Police Station.

Ahmed's assistant led me to the doorway, where the melee was well under way. An explosion of human emotions raged out of control, as the two guides battled their cases before the police. I entered the room and stood near the only empty chair, expressionless, as I quietly observed.

I never sat down, holding my position.

To my left was one of the members of my group, one of the two "witnesses"... then Laura, and next to her was seated the Chief of Police. His assistant sat to his left, furiously taking notes. As I scanned the room, I saw the tourist policeman who had been present at Karnak, another armed police representative to his left, and then a formidable character, some sort of militiaman, sitting behind the biggest desk in the room. Moving past his desk with my eyes, I saw the outraged tour guide seated next to him, screaming and kicking and fighting for his dignity. Another man—sitting to his left, a quiet participant—appeared to be some form of legal counsel.

To my right was Ahmed, red-faced, defensively fighting for his rights, but clearly losing ground. The second member of my group to be brought in as a "witness" sat next to him, closing the circle. I looked back at Laura, slumped down in her chair. She looked as if she were attempting to make sense of what her command performance had created, now that the situation had become so blown out of proportion.

She looked back, as if to say, "This is what I get for trying to help!"

Although I do not speak a word of Arabic, it was not difficult to understand the conversation. The tour guide was arguing that he never touched Laura and that Ahmed had created this diversion to protect himself from eventual issues with the tourist police. He had truth on his side.

Ahmed was screaming that the man had sexually offended a foreign tourist, hoping to deflect the attention away from the real issue. It was a lie. He knew it, Laura knew it, and so did the guide.

As I stood there near the entranceway, peering into the dark room, I felt an unrecognizable force rising within me and screaming to take command—the fire of Sekhmet. I stood my ground and asked to speak. Ahmed, fearful that I would only aggravate the situation, tried to override my request and kept talking. Calmly, but firmly, I asked again. He overrode again, motioning me to let him handle the situation, which he clearly was not handling well at that point.

Finally, as the situation reached near physical violence, I broke right through the crazed arena of screaming Egyptian men and walked directly across the room to the farthest policeman, so that I was actually cutting the circle of polarized energy in half. In the midst of this craziness, I had the audacity to interrupt the proceedings by asking for a cigarette—an unthinkable action for a woman in that culture and even more out of place in that situation. This broke the energy momentarily, as they all reacted to what was, for them, clearly inappropriate—I dare say "outlandish"—behavior.

I painstakingly drew the cigarette from the pack, taking time for everyone to exhale, and felt all eyes fixated upon me.

I asked him to light the cigarette for me and then, dramatically, took a puff, looking back at the circle of fire.

Imagine? Can you imagine a room filled with that intense Arab male energy, a cacophony of testosterone in overdrive, and the impact of that simple action?

Slowly and deliberately, I walked back to my chair, having created enough of a diversion that a shift in the intense emotions that had been driving the conflict was now palpable. But I did not sit. I stood there, cigarette in hand, demanding (in a much louder, more authoritative voice) that I be allowed to speak, and finally was granted my turn, with Ahmed acting as my translator.

I made eye contact with everyone in the room, acknowledging them all, aware that I was being tested, knowing that in the subtle ways of spirit, this was all part of yet another great initiation.

After introducing myself as the leader of the group, I faced the one I had identified as the Chief of Police, cognizant of the fact that one mistake could aggravate the case against Ahmed.

I spoke my piece: "You, sir," I said firmly, "find yourself in the middle of a conflict that I have created."

Ahmed translated and the room fell silent as all were shocked to hear that, in a room filled with finger-pointing, accusatory men, here came a woman, a foreigner, with the courage and presence to fearlessly declare herself the "guilty party."

I took another dramatic puff of the cigarette, sure of its theatrical impact, and continued: "I am the responsible person here," I said. "This is **my** group, and I should have been there, to explain to this man why we were holding up the entrance to the temple." I pointed to the tour guide.

"So, if you are going to put someone in jail," I said, almost defiantly, "it should be me."

The Chief looked at me, unbelievingly, making eye contact with every male in the room. He puffed his cigar and muttered something in Arabic, which Ahmed translated: "Were you doing a meditation there?" he asked, clearly disapproving. The Egyptians, most of whom are strict Moslems, do not welcome our form of spiritual worship in what they consider their "pagan" sites. This is particularly true now that people of the Islamic faith feel as though they have been wrongfully stereotyped by the Western world.

"Yes," my decisive reply.

My eyes drifted for a moment to Laura, who looked back at me in relief. She knew I was in my power, with Sekhmet rising . . . about to raise the roof.

"Did you have permission from the Department of Antiquities?" he retorted. I glanced over at the tour guide, who was grinning ear to ear, knowing he had the momentum and that he was about to be vindicated.

"No, sir," I answered succinctly, "we did not obtain permission."

"Do you understand that this is forbidden?" he pressed.

Ahmed looked at me as if to say: "Thank you . . . this is where they take me off to jail."

At that moment, the Sekhmet fire rolled through me like lightning. Without even answering the Chief . . . without acknowledging his question, I turned to the guide and asked: "What are we doing here?"

He looked at me suspiciously, trying to calculate my next move.

I was unwavering.

"How is it," I asked, motioning to him and to Ahmed as well, "that something so beautiful and so important as you both do, helping people discover the beauty of Egypt, has reduced good people to such violent and inhumane behavior?"

The guide looked at me quizzically, as if to say, "Who in the world are you, anyway?"

"You are the custodians, true . . . but Egypt is the heritage of all humankind," I said, gesturing to all the individuals in the station. "All of us. . . .."

I fixed my attention upon him.

"Surely you understand what great emotion is unleashed within people when they finally stand before the icons of the world's greatest civilization, don't you?"

He nodded begrudgingly.

"You, sir," I said to him, "are in your right to be angry and vengeful. You have been accused of less than honorable behavior and I understand that you must defend that honor."

His smile was cautious, but smug.

"You are my teacher," I said, humbly. "To you I ask for tolerance and forgiveness."

From my peripheral vision, I caught a glimpse of Ahmed, who was speechless.

"You, Ahmed, have handled this situation poorly," I said. "You are guilty of a lack of judgment." I took one last dramatic drag from the poisonous prop, the cigarette, and turned my attention back to the Chief of Police.

"You, sir, are faced with upholding the law and I have clearly broken it by not paying these necessary fees for the permit in question," I said. "You have every right to arrest me and charge me for this action," I said flatly.

The men darted glances at each other around the circle, not knowing what to make of this rather dramatic turn of events.

I stood in the doorway, blocking the only natural light from outside, as it cast a tall shadow across the room.

"Someone has to be wrong here and in this system, someone is going to get hurt," I said. "Look around. It seems you all really want someone to get hurt here—and for what? What terrible wrong has been committed to bring you to this? Isn't it absurd that you have come to such rage over something as insignificant as this?"

I made slow and deliberate eye contact with each of the police officials.

"Now I ask you, gentlemen, can't we do better than this?"

I walked over to the guide and asked him to stand up and to give me a hug. No one breathed. He stood up and, despite all the cultural barriers, despite everything that had happened, he hugged me—and I hugged him back.

Again I said to all present, "Can't we be better than this?"

As we stood there, embraced—one human being to another— he whispered in my ear: "I would never have touched that woman improperly. It's a lie—I want you to know that." He had tears in his eyes and didn't try to hide them from me.

I embraced him even more tightly and whispered back, "Can you forgive it?"

As the incredulous police stared in disbelief, I asked Laura to come and hug him and to forgive the incident. Resistant at first, they finally hugged, breaking all the rules, all taboo, and together, in that incredibly honest moment, we all shifted to a new vision of what we can achieve when we are just human, in truth and forgiveness, overriding the darkness of vengeance, ego, and rage.

I looked back again at the Chief of Police.

"We can be better than this," I reiterated. "We just need to talk to each other, instead of fighting **all** the time. We can go to that higher place, that goodness that we all are capable of and we can override these lower emotions. We can go to a place of compassion and understanding, and be better human beings ... much better beings ... much better than this."

I looked directly into the eyes of the Chief and he looked into mine.

"Can't we?" I asked, imploringly, almost a whisper now.

Visibly moved, he stood up.

"Yes! Yes, we can!" he said, triumphantly. "We **can** be this, Madam. We can be better than this!"

Spontaneously, everyone stood up and starting hugging each other. Something great had happened for us all—something monumental and yet, so simple. Ahmed looked at me in sheer amazement, unable to fully process what was happening but, in his eyes, I could see the recognition—the lesson he was bringing back from what he had seen come from Truth.

I asked Ahmed and the guide to forgive each other and, to the surprise of all, they too embraced, smacking each other on the back as men do in their male safety zones, and with that—the war ended.

I turned to the entrance, the light of the sun drenching the dingy, smoke-filled room in its inimitable energy, where I am sure that I saw Sekhmet's powerful presence bouncing the sun's rays off her strong shoulders and the crown of her lunar disk.

The radiance refracted around the room, touching everyone, as if we had all been knighted, and the brilliance at the doorway led us back into the pure light where souls reach new heights.

As we walked from the Police headquarters there in Luxor back to our docked cruise ship, I asked myself: "Are the gods of the Egyptian pantheon, more than ancient archetypes for the forces of the Universe, actually depictions of man in his higher state, evolved beyond the duality of the third dimension—ascended beings of our own Earth?"

∾ 7

Pantheon of the Gods

Returning to that earlier visit to Luxor in 2001, I remember so distinctly leaving the city with a private guide and driver and heading out for the Temple of Hatshepsut at Deir el-Bahri, intent upon deepening my contact with whomever or whatever had whispered to me from the winds that blew through the mighty pillars, there, in the sacred space of the Hathor shrine that lies within the temple grounds.

I had a sense of foreshadowing, so sure something quite remarkable was going to happen for me there—something that would bring me closer to understanding the buried memory of Hatetsesheti. Yet, at the same time, I felt an underlying resistance to opening that Pandora's box of repressed memories any more than I already had back in Boston.

∾

There is a trick to getting the most from visits to sacred sites and that is simply to get yourself out of bed before dawn, while the masses of tourists are still fast asleep in vacation mind, and to go to the temples before the hoards "wake up."

If your mission is of a spiritual intention, one of true inner exploration, you are going to want to experience the nuances of subtle energy, which elude the distracted and can escape your field of vision when your focus is blurred by the denser, slowed vibrations of others, who perhaps walk a different path: no less significant than yours, but of a different focus and intent.

To experience the subtle, etheric energies of ancient Egypt, you need to escape the noise of others, as you silence your own chattering mind of its distractions. You want to tune in to every layer and all the elements—the essence of consciousness that surrounds and permeates all things.

How else will you notice the beetle, messenger of spirit?

You want to hear the sand and the earth crunching below your feet, grounding you; to know the softness of a desert breeze caressing your cheek; to feel the spray of the Nile waters as you sail to other worlds; to pull the sun's fire into your core.

You want to "tune in" to the sublime.

This early-morning approach to sacred journeying requires discipline, admittedly, but that is when you really catch the magic of Egypt, when Ra is just returning from his journey through the underworld. It is in the rose-tinted shades of the sky at dawn that the third eye is most easily activated to perform as a kaleidoscope between the three-dimensional perception (where one perceives borders and outlines as the parameters of sight—the separation) and the ethereal, whereby the neurons of the brain are activated by the subtle energies penetrating and interacting between the dimensions—the entirety.

You change the focus and you see different forms, reflections of the brain's capacity to receive and process the multidimensional resonance frequencies that permeate all the layers. You see patterns of astral beings and thoughts and even other time frames, reflecting back at you from points upon the space-time continuum that are harmonious with where you are, in every sense.

It is as if the oblique light, hitting the earth at very specific angles, refracts in the divine lens of the inner eye, whereby you are enabled to see beyond the limitations of the three-dimensional perspectives of color saturation, density, and form.

We are always delighted (at times, even obsessive!) when our cameras pick up images that we may miss with our physical (even our psychic) eyes. The Internet is aglow with every kind of digital frame that appears to have captured spirits and orbs, reflecting other realms to us from that precise moment of exposure. These images can be and often are explained and dismissed as optical illusions and, as excited as we become when we find them hovering in our photos, we need to be discerning and ground our discoveries in objectivity.

Many of the images we see on our digital screens are indeed effects of light bouncing around, refracting in the lens.

Many others, however, cannot be explained away so easily.

What matters, in the end, is that we are **looking** now, like we have never looked before, and perhaps that desire to discover spirit is, of itself, the most important key to the **materialization** of spirits—both as psychic phenomena and as captured light forms in the new digital photos of our times.

Unquestionably, we are facilitated in our desire to connect with the spirit world when we take ourselves to the high-energy, sacred sites of this great planet.

Hakim speaks of the Land of the Sahara as the primary and central location on the planet, where the most powerful streams of cosmic energy enter, and he says that directly opposite Egypt, in Hawaii, is where they exit. This, he explains, is evidenced in the perennial flow of magma, which continually spills out from the Kilauea Volcano, across perpetually forming land masses and into the sea, where the island chain is in a perpetual state of being born anew.

Interestingly, this interpretation coincides with the channeled Sirian teachings, which pinpoint Egypt and the Big Island of Hawaii as two of the primary energy vortices of Gaia.

In my personal experience, there is no other place like Egypt to experience the manifestation of spirit, in so many different forms. When you are receptive to what surrounds you, you feel this constant sense of how the past is bleeding through the time lines, changing your perception of reality, impacting you in ways you cannot even understand.

Somehow, though, you know you are somewhere between sacred space and the higher dimensions, capable of downloading the ancient record. You know you are ready to receive imprints from other dimensions and other realities, perhaps from entire parallel universes, where we also exist, simultaneously—reflections in the cosmic lens.

Bear in mind that the motivation to get up just before dawn is often not enough—that will get you **to** the gates. Pockets full of baksheesh and the willingness to pay more than you bargained for, as well as knowing how to help the Egyptians bend the rules, are often what get you **through** them—so it is best to be prepared for that eventuality. If spirit manages it of itself, and the path is made clear before you effortlessly . . . all the better!

Once having accomplished the "tipping ceremony" (as I like to call it), I entered the temple grounds and just stood quietly near the entrance, drinking in the immense beauty of this incredible place.

There was not a sound . . . nothing to interrupt the calm serenity of that divine moment.

Only the call of birds, flying overhead, disturbed the silence, rippling, like the gentlest of waves, across the still waters of my mind. As I watched them, soaring over the temple in perfect geometric formation, my vision shifted, like that metaphorical kaleidoscope, and to my amazement, the jutting cliffs began to shape-shift into powerful images of Egyptian gods.

I blinked a few times, making sure I wasn't hallucinating.

Right at the top of what appears to be a triangular mound of rock face, I clearly saw an absolutely perfect image of Horus, the falcon god, the god of the sky—"He who is Above." His form was clearly defined in the rocky promontory, on high, overseeing the valley where Pharaoh Hatshepsut chose to pass to the beyond. *See Frame 12.*

In the pre-dawn lights of the illuminated temple, Ma'at, the goddess of universal truth, reigned over Hatshepsut's temple with majesty. Her image there is the perfect depiction one sees in the hieroglyphic writings of the ancients, as she reigns, in final judgment, over the souls of pharaohs past.

There, so prominently positioned above the funeral complex, she seems to forever guard over the soul of Hatshepsut. *See Frames 13A, 13B, and 13C.*

As the cliffs blushed in the pink light of dawn, other shapes seemed to jump out from the sandstone and the gods of Egypt began to reveal themselves to me.

I do see them with both the physical eye and the inner or "psychic" eye—but I have never before shared this publicly. Until the writing of this book, I had mentioned the visions, ever so briefly, only to Hakim—years ago—asking him if it was my imagination, or was there a fabulous image of Horus carved into the rocks behind Hatshepsut's temple.

He looked surprised, but pleased with my observation, and nodded his acknowledgment.

"Excellent," was all he said about it.

The question surfaces in my mind: might this incredible mountain have actually been sculpted, perhaps by giants, in the images of super beings or gods who once walked those sands, perhaps even before the Atlanteans, the Khemitians, and the pharaohs? Could these have been representations of alien beings, left tens ... even hundreds of thousands of years ago?

Or could the evolved beings represented in the symbols be manifesting these images from other dimensions, shifting in and out of the viewer's consciousness, via the rocks of the great valley of passing?

In the eyes of the distracted, perhaps, the focus at the valley remains locked upon the glorious temple of Hatshepsut, the sculptures and the fanfare of pharaonic grandeur, while the majesty of nature itself and the great rock sculptures seem to have been washed away in time.

Through my eyes, however, it is what lies behind the temple complex, the Pantheon of Gods, that provides the truest memorial to a spiritual treasury of such immense proportions that it is almost impossible to free the mind enough to allow what is there to penetrate and to see what is just barely clinging to the cliffs.

In my mind, there remains a great enigma here: how this incredible shape-shifting mountain could escape the vision of fellow journeyers. Until just days ago, in perfect synchronicity with the writing of this specific chapter, the only validation (of the human variety) I have ever had that the Pantheon of the Gods of Deir el-Bahri is far more than a figment of what some die-hard skeptics call my "fertile imagination" was that knowing smile from the wisdom keeper, Hakim.

The great master teacher that he is, he encouraged me to pursue these discoveries, as if I were opening a new hall of learning and, for years, I have returned again and again to the mysterious Temple of Hatshepsut to explore this field of shifting dimensions, recognizing the mountain as the passageway from which the gods and, perhaps, enlightened mortals escaped and returned from the spirit world to the material . . . and back again.

At times, I feel compelled to just walk up to the mountain's edge, defying the guards, and simply walk through the rock to another world. On some very deep, ancestral level—I seem to know I **can.**

Just days ago, I was excited to come across the Web site of a fellow mystic, Debbie Johnson, who has seen the same visions, made the same observations, and felt the same wonder as I have, at the sight of what she calls the "simulacra" at Deir el-Bahri. It was a celebration to discover a kindred spirit in Debbie, whose visions and experiences of the place so closely parallel my own.

Her Web site is rich with information and images, whereby the viewer can explore the phenomenon through sketches over the photographed areas of the mountain, where the forms appear.

It is not as powerful as being there, of course, but nonetheless through Debbie's efforts at rendering the images via her site, one can have a first encounter with this phenomenon.

Of the gods and goddesses appearing in the rocks, she writes:

This is the land of the Gods literally, and many of the God forms that are expressed within the text and art of the ancient Egyptian myths appear in the rock formations on the valley walls. The mountains and valleys of Luxor's West Bank challenge one to participate with nature in creating a vision that belonged to the ancient ones.

Perhaps the mystery held within the text and art has been available to us for some time, waiting to be noticed with higher consciousness and vision. The visual perspective is simple and obvious for those with a creative imagination and if one is cluttered with predetermined details, awed by temples, statues, and tombs, one might forget to look around at the beauty that nature has to show in this area.

It is possible that the rock formations of Western Thebes as well as the contours of the horizons hold the key to the ancient spiritual and philosophical system. These forgotten Gods are perhaps even the original spark of creation that ensued the myths of the local Egyptian deities in the time of Zep Tepi, the first time. These images give one a new perspective and understanding where the creative dream world inside the mind takes flight.

If one pays close attention to the limestone hillside at Deir el-Bahri, this amphitheater of weathered and rounded shapes takes on forms of the Egyptian Gods. The Deir el-Bahri amphitheater has been the preferred location for temples and tombs since the beginning of occupation in Upper Egypt. These hillside images were most likely the reason why they chose to build on the West Bank as well as opposite this mountain on the East Bank. The desire to protect and serve their god images, to see them each day, and to be near them in death all played a part in the temple locations.

These godly images on the mountain can be connected to known Egyptian Gods, Goddesses, and familiar ancient symbolism within *the recorded myths. The identification of specific Duat characters is amazing, in that specific deities occur together on the mountain, as well, their characters interact with each other within mythical records.*[6]

—Debbie Johnson

Sharing this monumental discovery with Debbie Johnson has sparked some exciting discussions between us as to the significance of our mutual discoveries, at this time in our personal and collective evolution.

Both of us see and experience the spiritual nature of what our industrialized societies, subjects of the Age of Reason, have long considered "inanimate" objects. Just as with the statues of Ptah and Sekhmet, the visionary connects with the vibratory essence of all creation—from the density of stone and mineral, to the highest realms of consciousness.

As we move into the new light of *Khepre,* the Age of Awakening, we are connecting, once again, with the consciousness of our Earth, knowing her as a living entity, just as we are remembering the stars as conscious beings. In essence, we are regaining the capacity to see beyond the veils of illusion and connect at the cellular, even subatomic level with the essence of spirit laced throughout all experience.

The Egyptians and other indigenous people held the wisdom of the Cosmos. They identified the physical passageways from matter to spirit ... the return from dust to stardust, perhaps?

There, at Deir el-Bahri, an active vortex between the dimensions still, to this day, reveals the nature of spirit to us—although

---

[6]Debbie Johnson, http://egyptianepiphany.homestead.com/index.html.

it still escapes people whose focus is elsewhere. I doubt it escaped the pharaohs, though, who chose the valleys adjacent to this mountain as the perfect place to rest their physical bodies in preparation for the soul's resurrection into eternal life.

～ 8

The Ennead of Creation

Whether the "neteru" (aspects of the Supreme Deity, named the "Atum" by the ancients) and their offspring were actually showing themselves to me as shape-shifting forms emerging from the rocky cliffs above the valley of the dead pharaohs of Egypt, or whether what I was seeing was an expression of my own mind moving in and out of different "frameworks" of consciousness, I knew it was happening because the gods had something to teach me. It was clear that what I would learn from them would be of incredible significance to my pursuit of the Secret Wisdom, disguised to the uninitiated, in the Egyptian fields of multidimensional reality.

Appearing to me there, almost leaping out from the immense sandstone precipice, the neteru of Egypt were saying: *"To see us is to know us. To know us, is to know thyself."*

There, high above the incredible temple grounds of Hatshepsut, they were reiterating the timeworn message of the Eleusian mystery schools.

My exploration of the gods of ancient Egypt began with an attempt to unravel creation myths of our recorded history and beyond, wondering how they have all reflected into our contemporary experience the profound beliefs of former civilizations, such as those of the Khemitian tribes of Africa, and those of the mythical (or shall we say the yet "unproven") cultures of Lemuria and Atlantis, which still float across the inner eye of forgotten memory.

Beyond my own awakening memories of Atlantis, I was eager to catch glimpses of this mystical land, woven through the time lines of the earliest Egyptian civilizations and, hopefully, to help to raise Atlantis from the deep sea burial grounds of our dormant collective memory, onto the steady ground of a far more distinctively "possible" reality.

From the native tribes of Alaska to the indigenous people of Zanzibar, every civilization on this planet is rooted in a primordial belief structure about how this world came into being: whether through religious texts, carved in stone, or carried through the oral tradition. Inevitably, the subconscious memory, reflecting back to us the Akashic Record of all experience (even our very species consciousness), holds the record of a cosmic sea—chaos—from which a mountain, primeval and without precedents, emerges.

I always marvel at the absolute incongruity of this universal description of a cosmic sea, described as "nothingness" from which Creation is born, as we unceasingly attempt to describe a beginning—a Big Bang—that triggered all that exists. For, what is a sea—from which all Creation is birthed? Isn't the sea itself a manifestation of Creation ... and a glorious one, at that?

How can we embrace the idea that a sea of nothingness, a void, existed **before** God, the Prime Creator? The idea of a state of nonexistence, to someone, like me, who believes that there are no beginnings and no endings to the Cosmos, is an utterly impossible concept to embrace.

It is no wonder why human beings, throughout written history and surely beyond, have struggled to come to terms with this existential enigma.

The ancient Egyptians bring us some of the earliest recorded contemplations of this baffling philosophical conundrum. Their most widely accepted creation myths are first revealed through the Divine Ennead of Heliopolis, recorded in the most ancient body of Egyptian religious texts to be uncovered by the archeologists. These are the Pyramid Texts, located at the temple/pyramid site of Saqqara, carved on the sarcophagi and walls of the pyramids from the Fifth and Sixth Dynasties.

The Divine Ennead of Heliopolis is based upon a principle of nine original gods (all aspects of the one Creator) and their emergence from this primordial state of pre-existence, which the predynastic Egyptians did indeed perceive as a watery void . . . of chaos—the *Nun*.

These ancient hieroglyphic records, dated more than two thousand years before Christ, elaborate the early Egyptian vision of Creation, just as they painstakingly describe the process of resurrection that must be followed for the pharaoh to return to his home in the stars . . . even demanding help from the gods themselves, if necessary.

The idea of mortals demanding the gods to assist pharaohs in their passage "back to the stars" resonates with the possibility that the early pharaohs were, indeed, from other star systems and that the call to the gods was, rather, a call to their star brothers and sisters—that their passage back from the earthly realm be supervised and aided from realms beyond their three-dimensional viewing stations.

Researching material regarding the Ennead, I came across

Pyramid Text number 1655 (referred to as "utterance 1655"), which lists the gods/neteru of the Great Ennead and acknowledges Atum, said to have been Ptah's creation, as the "Father" of the other eight, who follow him. It reads:

> *O great Ennead, which is Heliopolis:*
> *Atum, Shu, Tefnut, Geb, Nut, Osiris, Isis, Set, Nephthys,*
> *children of Atum, extend his heart to his child, the King,*
> *in the name of Nine Bows.*

So many years after hearing the voice at Giza shout out from the heavens, "O Helios, open your bow!" this text came as a powerful validation. It enabled me, finally, to understand the significance of the heavenly message. I recognized then how it had been given to me as a key to unlocking the gates of some indecipherable layer of reality to which, it seemed, I had earned preliminary access.

Nun

Does this "watery void" describe the state of the Universe "before" God's creation, as is mirrored in almost all contemporary religious teachings: "In the beginning...The earth was formless and void, and darkness was over the surface of the deep" (Genesis 1:1–2)? Or could the universal tale be describing the Great Flood, when Atlantis sank deep below the seas and most of Earth's land mass was covered in water—circa 10,800 BC?

According to the Heliopolitan Ennead teachings, this is indeed referring to the "before" of existence and it is from these waters that a mound—the primordial mountain—rises.

It is known, in the Egyptian texts, as the "Benben."

It is from here, this vortex of immense energies, that the Father of all gods, the *Atum,* rises, giving form to chaos . . . creating the world.

At the eve of the new millennium, the Egyptian government, in collaboration with "key" world leaders, planned to place a representational golden cap, the Benben stone, over the Great Pyramid's apex point. The plan was thwarted at the last minute, supposedly because there was much resistance from the people of Egypt, who believed that this was some sort of Masonic ritual, which it surely appeared to be. Whether it was the outcry of the people at Giza or whether it may have had something to do with the light of Sirius, which was directly overhead at the Giza Meridian at that hour, we may never know for sure. What matters is that the plan was thwarted—and the light prevailed.

If the Great Pyramid is indeed the re-creation of the mound of creation, one can only wonder: had the Secret Government succeeded back then, when Sirius was directly aligned over Giza, what untold force might have been unleashed upon our contemporary, polarized world?

We may never know that either, but what we do know is that, despite their collective intention, they **could not** place the Benben stone on the Great Pyramid.

Period.

Never forget that, whenever your heart becomes weary and you feel lost in what **appears** to be a hopeless dimming of light to the darkness.

The first of the Ennead of Egyptian gods, precursor to the birth or creation of Earth herself, Atum, the explosive creative force, is also associated with Ra, the sun, and eventually becomes

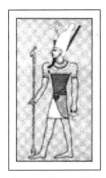

Atum; Atum-Ra

known in the mythology as "Atum-Re" or "Atum-Ra."

The Egyptian neter that most closely mirrors the Judeo-Christian concept of God, the Atum was understood to be "the perfection"— the god of all Creation: the Supreme Deity. Later myths place Ptah in that position and eventually merge the two aspects into one.

According to one of the many ancient Egyptian interpretations, Atum rose up from Nun, and spit out the first twin deities (described as "twins," as they were dual aspects of the element of air): Shu (the air) and Tefnut (the moisture).

Interpreting the metaphor of the "spit" of Atum as a fiery eruption (for he is associated with the element of fire), it is easy to recognize the mythological depiction of the birth of the Universe from a spark of primordial intelligence—the explosion of energy: Creation.

Fundamentally, this is the same explanation that physicists use to describe the Big Bang: the Universe sprang forward from that first atom (Atum?), which, exploding, disseminated all of its particles and frequencies throughout the receptive fields of the Cosmos. It, too, fits perfectly with the teachings of the Sirian High Council, who describe to us how, as sparks of Divine Light, we break away from Source to experience "I am" awareness.

Like lava from a mighty volcano, our spirit flows from the cosmic sea of All That Is into the waters of our earthly worlds— our bodies—in waves of immense brilliance!

Reflecting back on Hakim Awyan's description of Hawaii as the "output area" of cosmic energy, one recognizes immediately how the Creation myth plays itself out, unendingly, in our three-dimensional reality: from the waters, the volcanic mountains of earth emerge. Lava explodes as perpetual fire, creating new land-forms, as the molten mass finds its way back out to the sea. It reminds us, with such eloquence, that Creation is infinite (without beginning, without end) and that all existence is in a state of constant evolution . . . and revolution.

Consider the Great Pyramid (note that "pyramid," in Greek, means "fire in the middle"). Isn't it a perfect representation of the primeval mound from which Atum rose to shoot the fires of creation into manifesting the three-dimensional reality in which we currently reside? From such a perspective, it is not difficult to imagine how the Egyptians might have envisaged, in its construction, an earthly model of the mound of Atum, from which the highest initiates, beginning with the pharaohs, could have been similarly catapulted back to the spirit realm—the stars!

Surely the Greek philosophers were thinking along these lines when they gave the structure the name "pyramid."

Through time, Atum was worshipped not only as the father of the gods but also as the father of the pharaohs—the protector god of their ancient bloodlines, which, agreeing with Hakim, I propose were of stellar origins. How fascinating to learn that, in the Pyramid Texts, Atum is depicted lifting the dead pharaoh from his pyramid to the heavens, in order that he might be transformed into a star god, a return to his stellar home—the star systems of Sirius and Orion.

Were the ancient ones leaving a record of how we return to other star systems, or could it possibly be that we do actually **become** stars in some mysterious canopy, an illusion of swirling lights and energy masses, that merely **appears** to be a universe— a place of indefinable space and time?

What if that light we perceive as a star in the heavens is actually the light of one cell—the master cell—of every living being? Could it be that the veil of illusion has made us forget that the Universe that appears to exist beyond our realm of possibilities actually lies within?

~

As for the twin deities of Shu and Tefnut, their union created the earth god Geb and the sky goddess Nut.

All but Tefnut are depicted in this hieroglyph, which represents the Universe: Nut, the goddess of the sky, above; Shu, the air deity, holding up the sky; and Geb, the earth god, lying below.

Nut, Shu, and Geb

The Egyptians so depicted the "beginnings" of Creation through the elements: first there was the water, Nun, from which the fire, Atum-Re, spat out the air. From the air, Shu-Tefnut, was born the earth, Geb, and the sky, Nut.

Once the elements have been represented—the earth, seas, skies, and sun (in Atum-Re) defined—Osiris appears as the god of death and resurrection: Lord of the Underworld.

The legend of Osiris is complex and there are countless interpretations of his story, many conflicting. He was also perceived as having once been a ruler, in body, on Earth, who brought harmony and well-being to the ancient people of Egypt, reigning with his sister/wife, Isis, goddess of fertility and love.

Osiris

Throughout Egyptian history, Osiris is depicted with unusual green pigment for skin, interpreted by Egyptologists as a symbol of the color of rebirth and fertility. He wears the pharaonic white crown of Upper Egypt, surrounded by a plume on each side, and he holds the crook and flail of divine authority held by pharaohs. This symbolism apparently originated with Osiris, which could be interpreted as the ancient Egyptians' attempt to depict Osiris as having once been a physical being, the king of an earlier, pre-dynastic Egyptian civilization.

As the story goes, the immense popularity and successful rule of Osiris (together with his beloved queen, Isis) incense his brother, Set, who conspires against him.

The established mythological tale describes how Set secretly takes Osiris's measurements and has a beautifully adorned casket made to fit his body perfectly. During a great banquet, Set then tricks Osiris into lying down in the casket, supposedly intended as a gift for whomever fit inside it—not unlike Cinderella's slipper. Once Osiris enters the casket, Set seals it with molten lead and casts it into the Nile, where it drifts until it is caught in a cedar tree, condemning Osiris to a most horrible death by suffocation . . . and oblivion.

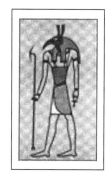

Set later finds the casket and proceeds to violently dismember the body of Osiris, strewing the body parts about to assure against the possibility that he can ever return to life in the physical realm: a truly gruesome murder story, filled with metaphysical allegory.

According to the myth, the goddess Isis transforms herself into a bird so that she can fly over Egypt, searching for all the pieces of

Set; Seth

Isis

her dead husband. She finds thirteen of the fourteen pieces, which she reconstructs into the form of a mummy. The missing piece, the penis, was said to have been swallowed by a fish, so she shapes a phallus out of the mud (earth) of the Nile (water) and places it on the mummy of Osiris, in preparation for her magic revival of her dead husband.

This magical resurrection of Osiris supposedly takes place at Abydos.

She spreads her wings and fans (air) the life back into him, stoking the inner flame (fire), until the phallus becomes erect—then she alights on it, and magically conceives Horus, their son, who later avenges his father's death.

This sacred moment is beautifully represented in the reliefs on the southern wall of the Chapel of Sokar-Osiris at Abydos. *See Frame 14.*

To accomplish this miracle, Isis is assisted by her sister, Nephthys (from the Egyptian name "Nebt-het," which the classicists define as meaning "Mistress of the House"), the wife of Set. Despite her marital union with the evil Set, she is loyal to her sister Isis and brother Osiris and so assists Isis in the magic that will bring Osiris back to life, for that moment of copulation, in order to bear Isis her son, Horus.

Osiris, in his mummified form, lives on as the Lord of the Underworld. Horus, his avenger, becomes the ruler of the living; the evil Set is condemned to a life of chaos and darkness; and Isis, mother of Horus, oversees the reign of her son.

The debate rages on among scholars and metaphysicians: were Osiris and Isis royalty of the Atlantean kingdom, bringing their light and wisdom to Egypt to rebirth a dying civilization? Did Osiris, a super mortal among men, great king and humanitarian, die from the hand of his brother, a deranged murderer, glorified in his death as "Lord of the Underworld"?

Or is he the deification of the process itself, the passing, whereby in death we reach immortality? Is Osiris the metaphorical embodiment of that most important aspect of mortal existence—the passing from the density, through the haze between the realms, the Duat, into the light of higher dimensions?

The Egyptians associated Isis with the Sirian star Sothis—the blue-white star that shines boldly on the winter horizon of the northern hemisphere of our celestial night skies. They linked Osiris with Sirius B, Satais, the ascended star now holding frequency on the sixth dimension, the source of the messages I receive from the Speakers.

I believe that, rather than depicting a tale of super mortals from Atlantis, the Osiris myth is describing actual cosmic events—the same as those that have been elaborated in the works of *The Sirian Revelations*. The Khemitians, who preceded the Egyptians, had a profound understanding of the Sirian star system, and no doubt veiled it in terms the populace could embrace.

Myth tells how Osiris (Sirius B) is buried in a casket sealed with molten lead and later cut into pieces. Could this "molten lead" be describing some sort of plasma ejected from Sirius C during its ascension and catapulted into the body of Sirius B? If we imagine that this event causes the physical matter of Sirius B to explode as the star ascends, we would have a correlation with the story of how Osiris is then "cut into pieces."

Isis (Sirius A) gathers the pieces in order to be seeded with new life, birthing a son from that union. Are we being told that Sirius A was starseeded from Sirius B, before the ascension of that star, birthing a new consciousness within the star system of Sirius A?

Is the "Isis" our One Heart, from which we will sculpt from the black mud of Amun, the age of darkness from which we are passing, the trigger (the phallus of Osiris) that will raise humanity from the darkness into the light, so that we will birth a New Dawn?

And what of Sirius C, associated at times with Nephthys and at others with her son, Anubis? The Egyptians relegated both of these gods to the underworld as well—again, as with Sirius B (Osiris), an indication that they had moved to another level of consciousness.

According to the famous myth, Set was condemned to a life of darkness and chaos. Could it be that he is the depiction of Nebiru, the planet lost in a desperate struggle between Sirius and our central sun, Ra, after the planet Nebiru was ejected out of the ascension trajectory of Sirius C?

Nephthys

Nephthys, whose symbols include the crow and **skulls,** becomes associated with death and goes on, myth has it, to serve as a protector of the dead, although this appears to be a rather simplistic interpretation.

Wikipedia, the free encyclopedia on the Internet, describes Nephthys in very mysterious terms:

Nephthys is a goddess of undetermined origin, but contrary to many erroneous claims, her ancient Egyptian name did not, in any way, mean "Lady of the House," as if referring to an ordinary human home. She was not in any way to be identified with some notion of a "housewife," nor as the primary lady who ruled the common domestic household. This is a pervasive and egregious error, oft-repeated, in very many commentaries concerning this deity. Rather, her name means quite specifically, Lady of the [Temple] Enclosure.

This title (which seems to be more of an epithet, rather than a goddess-name) likely indicates the association of Nephthys with one particular temple or some specific aspect of the Egyptian temple that is now partially lost to modern understanding. We do know, from a wealth of sources . . ., that (along with her sister Isis) Nephthys represented the temple pylon or the great flagstaff heralding the Divine Dwelling. Due to her very streamlined role as a protective entity, we may even consider the simplest explanation in which Nephthys truly lives-up to her unique epithet and is to be identified with the fundamentally protective temple enclosure-wall itself. All other efforts to determine the exact origin of this goddess remain speculative. To reiterate, her name seems to be an epithet masking the original, sacred name of this divinity (whatever it was). Sacred names were kept secret.

—Wikipedia

In my book *Atlantis Rising,* the Sirians describe the Atlantean location of a Committee of Thirteen Crystal Skulls as the Temple of Nephthys (the "temple enclosure-wall itself," as stated in Wikipedia). Is it any wonder, reflecting on the hidden messages of myth, that her name would be an epithet masking the true identity of what was laid to secrecy by the ancients, assisted by light beings of other worlds . . . awaiting the awakening of humankind?

~

Some stories declare the scattered pieces of Osiris's dismembered body as "fourteen," others as "thirteen." This contradiction stems from two different aspects of the same story and needs clarification. According to mythology, Set cuts Osiris's body into fourteen parts, and then strews the pieces across the lands of the Khemit, but Isis finds only thirteen parts.

That Isis actually locates only thirteen parts of the body, and then creates a fourteenth, the phallus of Osiris, rings many bells for the metaphysical seeker. It resonates with the story of those thirteen crystal skulls of Atlantis, recounted in a wealth of myths handed down from various oral traditions and coming to the foreground of our consciousness now.

In *Atlantis Rising*, the Sirian Speakers describe how, of the thirteen crystal skulls of Atlantis (a complex multidimensional "computer" system gifted to humanity from the Sirian Elders), twelve were separated and carried to different places on the Earth, so that the ultimate power derived from their union would not fall into the hands of the dark warriors of the time: the Dark Brotherhood of Atlantis.

According to that text, the thirteenth skull, the Master, was deliberately de-materialized, its vibrational essence placed in a sort of multidimensional holographic field (the Ark of the Covenant, perhaps?), awaiting the successful reunion of the other twelve.

If we reread the Osiris myth with an eye to our modern technology, we recognize that the story depicts the creation of a holograph.

According to Wikipedia:

Holography (from the Greek -hólos whole + -graf? writing, drawing) is a technique that allows the light scattered from an object to be recorded and later reconstructed so that it appears as if the object is in the same position relative to the recording medium as it was when recorded. The image changes as the position and orientation of the viewing system changes in exactly the same way as if the object was still present, thus making the recorded image (hologram) appear three dimensional."

This very recent modern-day discovery of light technology describes, in technical terminology, how the reunion of the twelve Sirio-Atlantean crystal skulls will create the vibrational field into which the thirteenth skull will be enabled to rematerialize in three-dimensional density, reopening an immense portal upon the no-time, as we are entering a New Dawn, the "Khepre" of Hakim's tradition.

It would explain, in far more comprehensive terms than the mythical story of the Egyptian legend, how Isis managed to "revive" the body of Osiris, as if we are being shown how his "scattered light" held the memory of the entire form.

It would also explain, in a beautifully celestial sense, why the Sirians even created the crystal skulls, which they gifted to Earth to assist the super race of beings, *Homo sapiens,* the seed of other star systems. These incredible artifacts, aspects of the light of Osiris (enlightenment), were later "scattered" around the world, just as the thirteen pieces of the body of Osiris (the star of Satais) seeded the higher consciousness of Sirius B into the awakening body of its sister star, Sirius A (Isis).

The light of the entirety, the multidimensional "computer system," would be retained in each of the twelve units, even if they were scattered. The thirteenth skull, the skull of Osiris, is the hologram that is activated when these twelve are reunited, and all the memory is retrieved. And, by the gods, it is a perfect allegory for how the light codes of our original twelve DNA strands were scattered within us and are now being called back to their original functions, through the creation of newly forming conscious light streams, bringing us to recognition of our true legacy as a super race of light beings, guardians of the physical universe.

The Sirians tell us that the Annunaki of Nebiru were responsible for creating the electromagnetic disturbance that scattered our DNA, creating the so-called "junk DNA" within us. If we interpret Set to **be** the planet Nebiru, then it all fits.

We have the story of the seeding, the separation, and the reunion, through which we realize that when the twelve crystal skulls are reunited, the thirteenth will appear, bringing enlightenment to humankind . . . and when the twelve strands of our light-coded DNA are activated, reunited, we achieve enlightenment: Osiris, the Christ Energy, Divine Presence.

∾ 9
Twelve Gates to Immortality

The Egyptian Book of the Dead describes the Duat, or the "underworld," through which the solar disk, Ra, moves in darkness through twelve gates—interpreted by Egyptologists as "the twelve hours of the night," although such interpretations are constantly being debated. It is the same journey the soul of the pharaoh will take, on his passing from life in earthly form to Divine Life as a celestial light being—a star in the heavens.

At each gate, Ra is confronted with powerful forces, depicted as "demons of darkness," on his journey back overhead, where he reappears to illuminate the world, a demonstration of the ultimate force and infinite light of the gods.

It is interesting to note that, in hieroglyphs, the Duat is depicted as a five-pointed star within a circle, as shown above. No self-respecting metaphysician can overlook the fact that this symbol corresponds precisely with the Wiccan symbol of the pentagram and I was struck immediately by its magical significance.

When the human form is imposed on the five-pointed star, with each of the four limbs outstretched to the points and the head conjoined with the upper point, we are shown man as a star—man as the microcosm of the macrocosmic universe. This is the principle described in Hermes Trismegistus's famed Emerald Tablet: "As Above, so Below, and as Below, so Above."

Why is the glyph representing the Duat composed of a five-pointed star surrounded by a circle—and what hidden meaning is there for us to retrieve?

Initiates of the mystery school of Pythagoras viewed the pentagram as the symbol of perfection, based on its sacred geometrical aspects: its form is representative of the golden mean ratio and it embodies the dodecahedron (the fifth Platonic solid, representing the "ethers"), which is constructed of twelve identical pentagonal sides.

It seems that no matter where you look in the various mystical traditions, "twelve" continually reappears.

If you consider that the symbol of the Duat itself contains the information of the Pythagoreans and other spiritual traditions ("man" as a star, encircled in what the Wiccans describe as a "protective field"—the exalted form of the human being in spirit), you begin to consider that there are secret meanings woven through the story of the Duat that most likely have yet to be revealed.

The pharaohs believed that the soul, the Ba, would have to journey through the Duat after death in order to return to the stars, from where it had originally descended to the Earth, to take its place as a star in the night sky. It would have to pass through twelve gates, each one presenting challenges and dangers for the soul to overcome, on its way to purification and eventual resurrection.

The classicists tell us that Dua means "dawning" and that when written with the final "t," it actually means the "dawning eye." They explain the star in the symbol as representing the sun, after its completion through the twelve gates—but, again, I believe there are far deeper meanings buried in the symbol and the story of this mystical journey. In the magical, coded language of the text, there are suggestions of very different meanings to the Book of the Dead than those that have been established by Egyptologists old and new.

Let us begin with a review of the sacred number, twelve, to discover what synchronicities can be found throughout myth and magic—and the teachings of the Sirian High Council.

* There are twelve strands of DNA, not two, within us and the thirteenth element is the activated pineal gland. The ten strands of material that we are beginning to reactivate by reassembling the scattered genetic bits have lain dormant in us from the time of Annunaki intervention in our planet, described at length in the Sirian material.

* There are twelve crystal skulls—the thirteenth is the Master Skull, which is not currently manifest in physical form, but which is being held in a hologram, in hiding, until the time when the twelve skulls are reunited.

* There were twelve apostles—Jesus Christ was the light, the thirteenth—the Ascended Master.

* There were twelve knights at the Round Table with King Arthur.

* According to the Theosophists, there are actually twelve sacred planets revolving around our central sun: the thirteenth "heavenly body."

* There are twelve gates in the Duat, after which the soul ascends to take its place in the stars—the "dawning eye."

* Twelve serpent goddesses light the way through the darkness of the Duat. As we know that the serpent is often used as a symbol of energy in its waveforms, could this be a coded description of the light, or piezoelectric energy, passing from skull to skull?

* The final gate, the twelfth, is guarded by two cobras, the goddesses Isis and Nephthys. It opens to the emerging light.

This twelve-around-one construct reoccurs significantly in many aspects of our lives, much of which have been based on ancient beliefs and records, handed down through time.

There are twelve months in our year; the clock is arranged in a circle of twelve hours around a center dial. Even the pyramid, four sides of a three-sided triangular face (twelve sides total) is held up by a central base—the thirteenth.

I found this synchronicity between the text describing the Duat (the "dawning eye") and the information I have retrieved from the texts, searching to decode the hidden messages left to us by the ancient Egyptian record keepers. In the *Papyrus of Ani*, a segment of the Book of the Dead, I was intrigued to read the following transcription:

The secret roads of Amentet and the manner wherein this great god is being rowed along over the water therein in his boat to perform the plans of the gods of the Tuat, the gathering together (of them) by their names, the manifestation of their shapes (or forms) and secret hours, such are the things of which the secret representation of the Tuat is not known to men and women.

Whosoever shall make this image in writing, according to the representation of the same which is in the hidden things of the Tuat, at the South end of the Hidden Palace, and whosoever shall know them shall be in condition of one who awardeth offerings in abundance in the Tuat, and he shall be united to the offerings of the gods who are in the following of Osiris and his Parents shall make the offerings which are obligatory on the Earth.

The majesty of this great god sendeth forth words and he giveth divine offerings to (the gods of) the Tuat and he standeth up by them and they see him, and they have dominion over their Fields

and over the gifts made to them, and they effect their transforma-
tions by reason of the words which this great god hath spoken
unto them.

As I read this text, I replaced the term "the gods" with an image of the ancient Sirio-Atlantean crystal skulls and I heard a different story emerging from the hazy interpretations we have had until now.

Could the Egyptians have actually been speaking, in code, of the twelve crystal skulls that had been gifted to the Atlanteans by light beings from Sirius? Is that secret road to Amentet, a place of passing from the third dimension, found at the doorway to the Crystal Skull Committee, the "enclosure itself"—the Temple of Nephthys?

The text speaks of the "gathering of the gods of the Tuat" by their names, their manifestation of shapes, and their secret hours. Does this refer to each skull having a specific name, or sound vibration, that resonates with its physical manifestation in the third dimension—and is the "secret hour" a reference to the time of their reunion on Earth?

The Book of Gates actually gives us the names of each of the gates and these may very well be the names (or more importantly—the sound codes) for each of the skulls. The text tells us, in code, that the "**gathering together** of them by name are the things of which the secret representation of the Tuat is not known to men and women."

The text itself tells us that there is another, secret interpretation of the Duat that is not recorded—"not known to men and women," invalidating the more surface, obvious interpretations we have inherited from historical Egyptology.

It may very well be that the sounding of these names, or sound patterns, is the key to activating the twelve crystal skulls that will lead us to the thirteenth—the Master.

The gates are named as follows:

First Field:	Net-Ra
Second Gate:	Saa-Set
Third Gate:	Aqebi
Fourth Gate:	Tchetbi
Fifth Gate:	Teka-Hra
Sixth Gate:	Set-em-Ma'at-f
Seventh Gate:	Akha-En-Ma'at
Eighth Gate:	Set-hra
Ninth Gate:	Ab-ta
Tenth Gate:	Sethu
Eleventh Gate:	Am-netu-f
Twelfth Gate:	Sebi Reri

The Book of Gates is inscribed on the wall of the Temple of Sety I, in the corridor that leads out to the Osireion. That passageway is clearly not the original entrance to the ancient structure, which has never been found—although Omm Sety may have come close in her supernatural visions in the temple. Yet, it is fascinating that the twelve gates are depicted on that wall, as if Sety himself were trying to leave the clues to lead future Adepts through the Halls of Amenti and into the light of the stars.

The Book of Gates tells us that in the twelfth hour of the Duat, Ra arrives at a gate with "a mysterious entrance." Is this secret describing the Osireion, this so-called "Tomb of Osiris," a place of immense energy and even greater mysteries? Is that "mysterious entrance" alluded to in the Book of Gates a depiction of the multidimensional portal that holds the hologram of the thirteenth crystal skull—the Master Skull . . . the transformational Osiris?

10

The Nephthys Portal

Given these titillating thoughts as to the buried secrets in the Book of Gates, I found it more than prophetic to learn that the myth of the murder of Osiris places his head, the thirteenth piece of his body, in the Osireion at Abydos.

I became convinced of this idea:

The mysterious Osireion at Abydos, a megalithic enigma the Khemitians date as fifty thousand years old, actually could be the location that contains the holographic coordinates of the Master Skull (the "head of Osiris"). Is it just possible that the Master is about to take form there, beneath the perennial waters that seep into the Osireion, with their murky pools camouflaging an ancient secret, at the moment the twelve essential parts of the galactic computer network, the Crystal Skull Committee, are reassembled by Keepers of the Crystal Skulls around the world?

Embracing the idea that Osiris is actually a metaphor for the actual **passage** between worlds and dimensions and that Nephthys is the "hidden" doorway itself (she does, after all, guard the gate!), it seems all too clear to me that Abydos, and the Osireion (where the "head of Osiris" supposedly lies), hold at least one of the keys to the mystery of the crystal skulls.

Isn't it time we turn these mystical keys, unlocking the secret passageways ... entering through the "wormholes" of the dimensions themselves and into the no-time?

This important myth is an archetypal representation of our rebundling DNA, at a time when we are reactivating the dormant DNA fragments within us, to eventually return to full twelve-stranded light bodied beings.

It speaks to us of how Osiris (the passageway through dimensional realities) is achieved when we retrieve the scattered bits and pieces of our de-activated DNA (the mud)—metaphor of our final years of darkness here on Earth—by giving form to the template (the phallus), the electric male principle, in order to seed Isis (the womb), the female magnetic forces of Gaia, so that we can birth the Horus, the New Dawn of enlightened humanity?

If that is the case, does not the pharaoh dwell within each of us?

With the story guiding us to that "al-Khemical" moment, we need to locate the proverbial hidden skull of Osiris (the coordinates of that multidimensional hologram) before the transformational process can truly begin.

~

Referring again to the book *Atlantis Rising*, the Sirians indicate that the Crystal Skull Committee resided in the "Temple of Nephthys," which they tell us was located "deep within an amethyst grotto in the inner earth sanctuary of Yzhnüni worship."

What I glean from their description of this inner earth reference point is that it appears to correspond to the surface area known as the "Devil's Triangle," where for decades we have heard of ships and planes going crazy or even disappearing off the radar!

In the chapter "The Skull Committee" from *Atlantis Rising*, they state:

> *Although the Temple of Nephthys was drawn deep into the below of your world, beneath the sands of the Atlantic Ocean its crystalline form remains intact to this day. It remains one of the most powerful vortex points on your planet, where for countless decades ships and planes have vanished into the vapors. These mysterious events simply cannot be denied, for many official reports of the disappearance of military equipment, sea-faring craft, and entire crews have described, with great detail, their vanishing from radar controls from one second to another: a scientific "impossibility."*
>
> —Atlantis Rising

I knew that if the Sirian Speakers were giving us such a specific clue, then there would have to be a link, something tangible, that I could work with, and I set out to find it. Where to look? Gaia's energy grid lines, a plotting of the primary fields of this great planet, would surely provide guidelines to the modern-day seeker, as they clearly have to the ancients!

If the Temple of Nephthys lay below the ocean floor in the Bahamas, how would it be linked to Egypt?

A number of fascinating charts and grid maps have been created over the years, which utilize the sacred geometry of the Platonic solids and other geophysical reference points, as well as Earth's harmonic resonance peaks, to delineate the planet's energy lines and power points.

Exploring these resources, I came upon the planetary grid map designed by William Becker and Bethe Hagens in 1987, which based itself on earlier plots from Russian scientists. They anchored the map by centering it at the Great Pyramid, and then aligning it to the north and south axial poles of the planet, to provide an incredible graph of Earth's bio-electromagnetic systems.

Sure enough, there I found uncanny similarities in the locations of the Bermuda Triangle, which sits on the same northern latitudinal grid line as a primary point in the Atlantic Ridge, an uppermost northern point of the ancient Dogon peoples in western Africa, the Great Pyramid at Giza—and even Lhasa in Tibet!

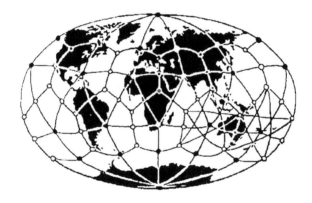

If you study the horizontal energy grid line that passes through Cairo (specifically through the Great Pyramid), you will be able to pinpoint the locations I have indicated above. Notice, too, that these points are triangulated with secondary power points on the planet, many of which are known as "vile vortices" of earth energy, and which are often the locations of ancient sites of worship. You will notice, for example, that Easter Island forms a cardinal point in a triangular energy pattern that links directly with the Devil's Triangle in the Bermudas.

I can already hear the skeptics screaming, from classic arche-ologists to the modernist interpreters of Egyptian history and myth, but here goes:

The following primary energy centers of Earth's northern lat-itudinal grid lines are all connected to each other, as they are to the Temple of Nephthys, via inner earth tunnels that all lead to Agharta, the inner world of the Earth, believed to be the home of a highly evolved, spiritually advanced civilization.

* The Bermuda Triangle (where the famed underwater Bimini Road, suggested as an ancient Atlantean roadway, is found)

* A point on the Atlantic Ridge known as the Atlantis Frac-ture, corresponding to a key location in Atlantis

* Northwest Africa, where the Dogon were located

* The Great Pyramid in Egypt

* The Himalayas between Lhasa and the Xi'an Pyramids of China

The "head" of Osiris, supposedly buried at the Osireion, is actually a metaphor for the master Atlantean crystal skull, the thirteenth, which was returned to the sixth dimension for safe-keeping, awaiting the reunion of the twelve that have been held in safe hiding, at the four corners of the world—as prophesied by the Maya. Its holographic imprint is located in the waters that flow below the temple, the Osireion, awaiting the electric "current," in a sense, that will be activated when the twelve are reunited by the Keepers of the Crystal Skulls, who will be shown how to locate the coordinates and send the frequencies of enlight-ened mind into the crystalline matrix of Gaia and the Greater Universe.

There has to be a direct correlation between the Osireion at Abydos and the Great Pyramid for this to work—and there is indeed.

Years ago, Hakim told me about a great underground river that the Khemitians believed had flowed to the west of the Nile for many millions of years. He described how this rich source of desperately needed water explained why oases spring up in the middle of the desert, explained in great detail in Stephen Mehler's book *The Land of Osiris.*

According to Stephen: "A report compiled from an international meeting of geologists in Egypt in 1963 provided information about the many observations and investigations by various geologists about the groundwater in the western desert. It stated that there was enough groundwater in the Western Desert of Egypt to supply all of the Middle East with fresh water for many years."[7]

When talking with Hakim about the connection between the Sphinx, the Great Pyramid, and the Osireion, he provided the key to understanding the missing link. The Khemitians, he explained, lived before the last Ice Age at 10,800 BC, which triggered the Earth Changes that brought desertification to the region of the Sahara.

They had enjoyed natural and man-made deviations of the ancient river that flowed at that time above and below ground throughout the entire continent.

The Sphinx and the Osireion were positioned very near the same riverbanks that linked Upper and Lower Egypt—and they served as gateways to the mystical world of the gods. This was

---

[7]Stephen Mehler, *The Land of Osiris* (Kempton, IL: Adventures Unlimited Press, 2002).

not the Nile. It was known to the Khemitians as the "Nir," which had dried up at the surface but which still today flows in the underground.

This would explain the true purpose of the great Solar Boat that was discovered in 1950, deep in a pit alongside the Great Pyramid by archeologist Kamal el-Mallakh, who worked for the Department of Egyptian Antiquities.

During work being undertaken there to clear the way for a road that would transport tourists through the Plateau, El Mallakh accidentally uncovered first huge blocks of limestone and later an airtight pit, in which the entire structure of an ancient wooden ship lay in thirteen piles of cedarwood slabs, ropes, and matting.

This magnificent find was painstakingly reassembled and now sits in its protective housing, right next to the Great Pyramid.

Most Egyptologists insist that the boat was never meant to be waterborne, but instead was representative of the Solar Boat depicting the pharaoh's journey through the Duat.

This is hardly credible when you observe that there are similar pits all over the Giza Plateau and that other boat parts have been discovered there. It seems to me that the Plateau was a great harbor, from which ships sailed the ancient river—most likely to one of their most revered ports, at Abydos.

Back in 1991, an American archeology team led by David O'Conner discovered **twelve** of these boat pits at Shunet el-Zebib, a funerary enclosure at Abydos. In each of these pits, the team discovered remains of wooden boats!

In dialogues I had held earlier with Hakim, he concurred that the underground river that he believes still flows below the sands of Egypt holds the memory and the frequencies of the Khemitian record.

It would make perfect sense that, for that reason, Osiris's body floated on the river of the Nir, the conduit, retaining the memory and the Light.

Is this the same source of water that perpetually ebbs and flows in the great Osireion?

∾ 11

Return to Abydos

I visited Abydos again in March 2004 when I returned to prepare the way for the SoulQuest™ spirit journey that I conducted later, in the fall of 2005.

I willingly braved the unpleasant convoy, the drama of police and checkpoints, and all the nonsense that one has to go through to get to the sacred village, eager to return. I knew that something remarkable—what I can only describe as a "homecoming"—awaited.

I understood a lot more by then, realizing why I had not entered the temple on my first visit. Clearly, its magic would have been lost to me the first time around: before reaching a deeper resonance with Egypt; before acquiring that basic foundation upon which one builds experience; before exploring the neteru, the aspects of the One God—those aspects of our own divinity.

I still had not stepped foot in the Temple of Sety I, nor in the great Osireion, which would eventually serve as my inspiration for the writing of this book.

I wondered if Amir would still be there and if he would even remember me—a thought that evaporated in the thin desert air the minute I stepped off the bus.

There he stood, at the gateway to the Cafeteria, greeting the tourists as they poured out of the convoy buses. We recognized each other immediately. The years that had passed since that first encounter, mere grains of sand in the hourglass of so many lifetimes, disappeared, surrendering to the no-time of yet another reunion.

We hugged, as closely as a man and woman can touch in public without offending religion and tradition. Our embrace was absolutely pure of intent, genuine, and joyful—and once again I felt that amazing connection—old soul recovery.

"Why have you kept us waiting so long?" Amir asked, the warmth of his eyes reflecting the beauty of this mystical world. "Abydos has been waiting for you.. . ."

He motioned to one of the waiters, and invited me to join him for tea. Remembering how I loved the wonderful mint tea, he ordered it for both of us. It was as if our first meeting had been only hours before . . . as if we had resumed our conversation from that point of parting, without any sense of separation—any sense of having to reconnect what was already "connected."

The joy of being back in Abydos, there with Amir, was indescribable. I think we both knew the bond was as old as the temple was timeless.

In those moments, when I reencounter old souls who have walked with me, somewhere along the path of the soul, I always get a signal: a glint of pure ruby-colored light sparks from their left eye, telling me, "Yes, it is me . . . do you remember?"

With Amir, it was more like a rainbow—full spectrum.

Within minutes, one of the boys brought the tea. Most tourists refuse to drink tea with the locals, fearing God knows what bionic bacteria lurk in the sediments. For me, it is so sweet, so Egypt . . . so ancient: a very special ritual.

Amir drank the boiling tea from his glass in one gulp.

"You are ready, now, to enter the temple?" he asked. There was a distinct air of mystery laced into the words.

"Not yet," I replied, marveling, in fact, at how I was now in Abydos for a second time, within footsteps of the temple I had come to explore, and yet had still not entered its holy walls. It was almost as if I couldn't bear to enter there now, for fear I would disturb the reverie of some ancient memory.

"Come," he urged. "It is time I show you some of the secrets of Abydos."

I jumped to my feet and followed Amir as he signaled to one of his helpers to take over at the Cafeteria, while he led me, like the Pied Piper, past the pathway and up to the entrance gate that opens onto the temple grounds.

We walked in reverence and silence, as if we had walked that ceremonial procession up to the courtyard of Sety I just that way . . . so many lifetimes before.

I remember so succinctly how the police and tourist guards acknowledged him, with such esteem, as he proceeded through the entrance, waving me through behind him.

I followed him through the outer courtyard and into the temple in an almost ceremonial procession: Amir ahead, giving the appropriate signs to the numerous guards, me behind, an acceptable distance from him—*The Priestess and the Keeper of the Gates.*

It was perfect, timeless, and ancient as the sands of time.

And it had happened before, just that way, only we had been dressed in the softest Egyptian white linen robes . . . back then.

∽

Amir lit incense he had brought for the gods as he reached the entrance.

I removed my shoes, barefoot for the first time in any Egyptian temple, and followed him in. The cool marble stones were smooth and refreshing, after the glaring heat of the desert sun, and I loved the feel of them under my feet.

It felt so right to have entered in that way: a barefoot pilgrim, humble before the gods.

The presence of others inside the temple became irrelevant, almost imperceptible, as Amir led me through the magnificent hypostyle halls, and then slowly, one by one, through the first six primary chambers, each a ceremonial temple to one of the neteru. The seventh Sety dedicated to himself, a temple to his own godliness, as if he were placing himself on a par with the gods.

At the back of the temple, one finds the sacred chapels of Isis, Horus, and Osiris. They are containers of some of the most powerful energies I have ever experienced in Abydos and would hold the key to some of the most important of my discoveries there.

At every turn, the sunlight filtered through the openings overhead, streaming in, softly, as if Ra himself were guiding me to the magic of ancient days.

It is a procession that requires days, weeks, even months to experience—surely more than the time I could dedicate then. I knew I would return, over and over again, in the years to come.

No other temple in Egypt, however majestic or imposing, fills the heart with the love that pours from Sety's temple at Abydos. Here Omm Sety spent the most important years of her life, walking barefoot the cool, smooth stones of this magnificent temple to the gods, remembering her lifetime as the Priestess Bentreshyt and her desperate love for her pharaoh.

Everywhere, it seemed, she was smiling through the ethers, gently nudging us into special spaces, guiding us to "remember."

Indeed, if you can reach that ultimate stillness within, you can sense her presence about you. There, in sacred Abydos, you can hear her laughter and feel her heart rejoicing.

Skillfully maneuvered away from the tourists and into the power spots of the temple, I experienced millennia of worship and devotion emanating from the walls, powerful energies rolling over my being, like winter wind on new fields of grain. The sweetness of that first encounter, and the blessings that I received then, have been etched on my soul . . . with the same exquisite expression as that depicted in the faces and postures of the deities carved into those magnificent frescoed walls.

Amir and I moved in such deep silence, detached from the sensate world, almost floating on the air of ages. The breathtaking art of ancient worshippers, the priesthood and pharaohs, spoke to my heart, revealing so many secrets.

Nothing could have disturbed the beauty and wonder of that first time entering the great halls, or shall I say the first time in this lifetime? For there was no question, from the moment my feet touched ground in Abydos, that this was my spiritual home.

The Temple of Sety I is unquestionably the most artistically elaborate and spiritually profound of all the archeological sites of Egypt. No doubt, we have Omm Sety to thank for basically dedicating her life to its restoration—from the crumbling state of disregard in which it stood, roofless and abandoned (and no doubt sacked of so many of its treasures), until she was transferred there by the Department of Egyptian Antiquities back in 1956.

Aside from its unique L-shape formation, the temple has other unique characteristics. The most significant is that it features these "Seven Vaulted Chapels," as they are described in her book, each honoring one of the neteru, with the exception of that seventh chapel that Sety dedicated to himself. These correspond, in order (from the right side of the building to the left), to the primary gods, as follows:

1. *Chapel of Horus:* son of Isis and Osiris, believed to be the protector of the living pharaoh and of Egypt

2. *Chapel of Isis:* wife of Osiris, mother of Horus, she was the goddess of love.

3. *Chapel of Osiris:* Lord of the Underworld

4. *Chapel of Amon Ra:* Creator God, first of the Ennead, considered the King of the Gods

5. *Chapel of Ra-Hor-akhty:* the evolution and union of the two gods Horus (god of the sky) and Ra (god of the sun)

6. *Chapel of Ptah:* considered to be the quintessential Creator God, the primeval mound itself, from which Amun-Ra sprang: he "spoke the word" and the world came into being.

7. *Chapel of Sety:* the worship chamber to the deified Sety

Inside each of these beautifully adorned chapels, which were dedicated to daily cult worship of the neteru by the priests and priestesses, there lies (at the wall facing west) a "false" sandstone door—representing the portal between earthly reality and other dimensions.

I would find out, soon enough, that they were still "fully operative"!

The Chapel of Osiris is the exception, as he was relegated to remain in the underworld—or, as I have alluded earlier, he **was** the passage, the transition, the doorway itself!

Worship involved placing offerings to the spirits of the gods at these doors, so that they might pass through the walls and enjoy the earthly offerings of fruits, bread, and beer that had been prepared for them. This is so significant to an experience I would have years later, when I would manage to get myself locked inside the temple, alone, for hours after closing—to be alone with the gods . . . to know the power of the sacred darkness there.

In each of the chambers, the exquisite wall carvings show Sety I himself carrying out the rites of worship to each of the gods. The viewer is left wondering: is Sety depicting his rites of passage, from mortal to deity, or is this merely representative of the pharaoh's role as honorary High Priest of the temple?

Seven being the number of the primary chakras, I am convinced that the design of these extraordinary chapels, and the daily worship in each, was also intended to serve to heal and align the chakric centers of the human form as part of a perennial initiation into the mysteries, which include the seven Hermetic principles—and these, too, have their correspondences in the neteru of the seven chapels.

They represent, as well, a musical octave.

Consider these mystery school teachings of Hermes Trismegistus—Thoth—god of wisdom in the Egyptian pantheon, known as the "Hermetic principles," the quintessential wisdom of the Khemitians:

 * **Mentalism:** *The All is mind—the Universe is mental.* **Amun-Ra**

* **Correspondence:** *As above, so below and as below, so above.* **Osiris**

* **Vibration:** *Nothing rests, everything moves, everything vibrates.* **Ptah**

* **Polarity:** *Everything is dual, like and unlike are the same.* **Ra-Hor-akhty**

* **Rhythm:** *Everything flows out and in; all things rise and fall.* **Horus**

* **Gender:** *Gender is in everything; everything has its masculine and feminine principle.* **Isis**

* **Cause and effect:** There are many planes of causation, but nothing escapes the law. *Sety I*

The mystery school teachings are built into the temple structure itself—they can be "read" by the student of esoteric wisdom.

This is the magic of Egypt. With so many thousands of years of consciousness woven into the ethers—so many worshippers and metaphysicians working with the energies of the sacred sites and power centers of so many civilizations—much is still intact, to be retrieved, by the Adept.

In the springtime of your spiritual climb, you can appreciate the artistry and love that have gone into the building of the temple. In the summer of your journey, you are able to attune to the vibrations and all that such sensitivity encompasses. In the autumn of your quest, you retrieve the coded wisdom and access other dimensions. In the winter of your passing, one imagines, you simply assimilate it all as the "One Heart," recognizing how all is a reflection of the All That Is, That Ever Was, and That Always Will Be.

In just one visit, there is not enough time to even begin to experience the entire temple—that is why I would return, over and over again, taking time to discover and embrace each message, each form, and the energy embedded in those magnificent walls.

It is almost more than the eye can cope with, more than the soul can bear—for it is so immense in scope and spiritual significance that you feel your mind struggling to process it all, while your heart expands beyond measure.

In perfect synchronicity with the mystical journey of discovery that guides me through this lifetime, the Universe perpetually provides beautiful, joyful confirmation at every juncture.

At this precise time of elaborating the spiritual significance of the number "seven," I have just been sent an e-mail from a friend and fellow crop circle investigator, Philippe Ullens, to which he has attached one of his aerial photos of an incredible crop circle, done this very morning at Eastfield in Avebury, in England.

This is occurring almost miraculously, as I write this text, on August 25, 2008.

I am astounded to see the formation of the seven-pointed star, the septagram (the quintessential symbol of alchemy), embedded in seven spirals of diminishing sized circles, which depict the Fibonacci sequence, described in sacred geometry.

What are the probabilities of such an occurrence? As I type the word "seven," a photo of a most beautiful crop circle, with the rare seven-pointed star, arrives through cyberspace?

These instant manifestations, sometimes, really boggle the

Philippe Ullens © 2008

mind. No matter how well you understand it all on the mental plane, it is still a wonder how everything knits together so perfectly, like a divine tapestry.

Where else does the seven-pointed star, the septagram, appear in Egyptian mythology?

Everywhere in the Temple of Sety, one finds depictions of a goddess who wears a crown bearing a seven-pointed star, covered by a crescent, possibly representing the moon. I gasped when I saw that she is dressed in a panther-skin, which resonates so powerfully for me through my shamanic journeys in the Native American and Mayan traditions, for the Panther is my power animal—and I have long known that I am of the Jaguar Clan.

And now, as I write about this goddess and her crown of the seven-pointed star, a crop circle appears in England and, thanks to Philippe Ullens, arrives at my desktop in absolute validation of all that is the magic and the wonder of Spirit!

This goddess of the seven-pointed star is often shown with Thoth, the god credited with the creation of hieroglyphs and writing itself, and scribe to the entire Pantheon of Gods. *See Frame 15.*

The Egyptians believed that without Thoth's words, the gods would not even have existed. He has also been associated with architecture, science, mathematics, and magic and is often depicted with Ma'at as the two gods who guide Ra's solar boat through the underworld.

The Greeks associated Thoth with their god Hermes, of similar attributes, and it is from that affiliation that he also became known as Hermes Trismegistus, or "three times great."

Later, when I did some investigations into the significance of Thoth, I learned he was a vital part of the Osiris myth. It was Thoth who gave Isis the magical words that would resurrect Osiris long enough to impregnate her so she could birth Horus.

At that time, without any knowledge as to who this goddess represented, I was struck by the fact that the headdress of the panther-clad goddess echoed the numerology of the seven chambers, knowing this held some higher significance as to the secrets of Sety's magic in which king, gods, and the temple itself form the trinity of exalted spirit.

As I walked through the temple, at times next to Amir, at others alone in silent exploration, this deity seemed to jump out at me from every corner, as if to say, "Look at me! I am important to you!"

I finally asked Amir who she was, in the Pantheon of the Gods, and what she represented.

"She is Seshet," Amir said, simply.

I looked at him in disbelief.

Thoth

Seshet; Seshat

"What?" I shrieked.

"Seshet," he repeated, seeming surprised at my strong reaction. "She is the goddess of writing."

My mind raced, like a flaming arrow, back to the regression and the name, "Hatet-sesheti."

"Are you sure?" I asked, visibly taken aback.

"Yes, sure!" Amir said, emphatically. He searched for the words in English that would allow him to explain what he knew to me in more detail.

"She is the helper to Thoth," he said, struggling to find the words. ". . . something like 'the recorder.'"

I literally took a step back, utterly amazed at what I had been given.

Later, back in Cairo, I would learn from one of the Egyptologists whom I know there that "Hat-et" means "the first: in feminine gender." When I asked him if there could be a specific meaning to the word "Hatetsesheti," my jaw almost broke **through** the floor when he said: "It means, in a female sense: the first of the writers, or the first of the record keepers . . . something like, 'the first of the women record keepers'. . . ."

I couldn't believe I had stumbled over the meaning of a name that had surfaced from the deepest waters of my subconscious mind and guided me to this moment, to Abydos, the heart of sacred Egypt. And what a name: "the first female record keeper"!

I almost spit on myself as I tried to speak, in the wake of what I was discovering.

". . . and what does Hatshepsut mean, then?"

He answered, "The first (or the highest) noble woman."

These new pieces of my multidimensional, "otherworldly" puzzle brought the picture into greater focus for me.

"Hatetsesheti" . . . had she been the *Keeper of the Records* to Hatshepsut—the pharaoh, Ma'atkara?

∞ 12

2005: The Sacred Journey

I finally led a group of spirit seekers on my first SoulQuest™ journey to Egypt in 2005. This intense program, a mission of initiation in the sacred sites of Egypt, began with a two-day workshop of DNA activation, which creates new harmonic resonance patterns within the cellular makeup—altering the intra- and inter-cellular waters, so that they vibrate at a higher intensity.

After those introductory two days of intense energy shifting and cellular regeneration, day three was dedicated to initiation inside the Great Pyramid, for which I had arranged two hours of private access for our group. During this extraordinary time inside the monumental construction, itself a resonance chamber for the stream of celestial waves spiraling into Giza, we would be fifty people in the tiny King's Chamber—the pharaohs' ascension gate—toning and chanting the music of our souls and anchoring the newly reassembled third DNA light filament in the greatest man-made earth energy station of the entire planet.

It would be a beautiful, memorable way to experience this reorganizing DNA material taking form, a perfect beginning for our sacred journey, and it would be powerful, to say the least.

The night before our pyramid visit, we enjoyed a fabulous dinner in a local restaurant, where a man was reading coffee cups—a form of divining. The ambiance was playful, and many of the group were having readings. Although I am rarely interested in being "read," I decided to contribute to the local economy and have my coffee cup session.

The reader turned the cup over and looked at me, somewhat awe-struck.

There, clearly evidenced—to perfection—was an image of Thoth, the ibis, sitting above a perfect pyramid—and below another, reversed! *See Frames 16A and 16B.*

He described what he saw as "Thoth appearing 'between the worlds'" and said he had never, in all the years he had been reading, ever seen anything like it—and suggested I had some strong connection to the god.

I looked at the cup and was, myself, amazed at how perfectly the ibis was represented in the coffee grinds.

Mysteriously, the reader stared into my eyes and said: "He will appear to you in the pyramid.. . ."

After that, he declined all other requests for readings. He absolutely refused to accept payment for mine and quietly walked away, thanking me for his having been given the opportunity to see what he had seen. He said it was a sign from the gods.

I thought it was all very odd—but then, it was so very "Egypt."

I looked at the cup again and, fortunately, I thought the image was important enough to be recorded, so I snapped a shot of it. The photo, unaltered in any way, was perfectly clear and captures the ibis in nearly impossible detail.

The pyramids that surround it speak to one of the most important axioms attributed to Thoth (Hermes Trismegistus), which we know as the "Hermetic principle": As Below, So Above and As Above, So Below.

Like a master magician, Egypt kept teasing me with glimpses of what lay behind the veil, just out of sight, and what was perpetually being presented to me—right before my eyes. It seemed she was giving me answers to questions that had still not taken form in my mind.

It was more than clear, though, that Thoth, the ibis, most definitely was represented in the coffee grinds, big as life . . . symbolically positioned between the "below" and the "above."

Approaching the Great Pyramid with the group, I quietly evoked Thoth's image, asking him to appear to me—more powerfully than through symbols—and to help the spiritual seekers in my group to receive initiation.

I was asking for "more" and man, did I get it.

Despite my previous experiences inside the Great Pyramid, nothing could have prepared me for what would happen when I returned with my group. Once the formalities with guards at the entrance had been finalized, we passed through the entrance tunnel to where the stairs veer off to the right, leading to the Grand Gallery.

You first climb through a low-ceilinged passageway, which you can accomplish only by basically bending in half, while you make the climb. You then proceed to the spacious Gallery, where you scale wooden slats at either side of the open space until you reach the landing, outside of the King's Chamber. Once you reach that point, you almost have to crawl on all fours through the very low opening at the bottom of the famous entrance wall of the chamber in order to enter there.

I have done this on a few occasions, when I have been blessed to have private time in the Great Pyramid, and the adrenaline

151

rush has always made of it a moderately difficult climb, rendered insignificant before the majesty of the experience and by the sheer excitement of being there. In short, your body takes care of the practicalities of getting you there, while your uncontainable spirit is catapulted into the realm of distant stars and unknown dimensions.

However, it would not be that simple for me this time, leading a group of initiates, as it had been for me on previous occasions, when being there on my own bore a completely different responsibility than my coming as a spiritual master of fifty initiates.

Almost instantly, as we began climbing the first passageway, I became disoriented and began struggling for air, as I had in the tombs in the Valley of the Kings. Whereas before I had climbed the stairs relatively effortlessly (albeit with a few well-timed stops for catching my breath), I was now finding it absolutely daunting and just about impossible to make the climb.

I barely made it through the first part of the ascent, that low-ceilinged tunnel up to the entrance into the Grand Gallery. I was already gasping for air, feeling that there was no way I would make it up to the top—something I had never even considered in earlier visits. Had I been alone, I surely would have given up and turned back—something I have never done before any spiritual experience, which, at this point in my life, includes climbing in and out of pyramids, through jungles, across deserts, and everywhere in between...wherever spirit calls.

I soon realized that this was just as much a part of my personal initiation as it was a process of my responsibility to each of the souls who had come on the journey, and so I pushed myself to the limit to overcome the physical stress and the overwhelming sense of being deliberately "obstructed."

I pulled myself up the wooden slats of the tunnel, focusing my mind and commanding my body to provide the energy surge needed to make it.

Once I reached the Gallery, I stopped and looked around at the magnificence of its impeccable architecture, recognizing (for the first time) how clearly it represented an archetypal, galactic birthing canal! How many people on this Earth would ever experience such awesome beauty, I mused, encouraging myself to push on. To be there, driven to feel, to know, to learn the mysteries of ancients, was such a privilege and an honor.

To bring others to such an experience was an immensely important responsibility, filled with reverence and humility.

As I climbed the short ladder, which led to the stairway to the left side of the Gallery, it appeared to me that the stairs were becoming longer ... growing ... as if with every step I took, the pyramid's stairway grew another foot! It would be best compared to the ladder on a fire truck, which extends outward to reach the upper floors of burning buildings. I took a step, the steps grew a step ... and this strange sensation became the overwhelming experience, as if the pyramid were somehow taunting me, obstructing me, and testing me—to what end, I had yet to know.

Later, I would find out that my Egyptian tour guide, who had gone into the space known as the "Queen's Chamber," while we climbed up to the King's Chamber, had experienced the exact same sensation. He agitatedly described the tunnel into the chamber "growing longer and longer" while he was trying to crawl out, describing his process as a rite of passage before dying.

Mystified, he described it as something he had never before experienced in his years of entry with other groups.

This he recounted to me, breathlessly, when we returned from the ceremony, while he was still unaware that I had had the same experience, which I recognized as one of moving through other-dimensional frameworks, presented by the Great Pyramid itself.

Unquestionably, in that remarkable time of initiation, the pyramid was activating for us all, as it no doubt had done in ancient days, when pharaohs catapulted themselves into the stars to dream, to remember their starseed connections, and then to return home.

Breathless after the infinitely challenging climb up the stairs of the Gallery, I finally reached the rungs of the last ladder, which takes you up to the landing. I clutched it for dear life, feeling so inexplicably exhausted that I had to stop to gather myself together, before taking those last few steps.

I looked up and there, where there had been a landing, I now saw a solid granite wall! I looked in disbelief, but the landing was gone—all I could see was this impenetrable wall before me— just as solid as the walls of the pyramid themselves, appearing to me not as a "psychic" vision—but as solid, 3D stone.

I turned around to my assistant, Laura, for whom this was a first sacred journey with me, just as it was her first time in the Great Pyramid.

"There's a wall!" I whispered to her in disbelief, struggling with the layers of consciousness between what appears as 3D and what you can only imagine is some "otherworldly reality."

Laura looked at me, bewildered. Clearly, she didn't see it.

The group was lined up below me on the two stairways in the Grand Gallery, waiting for me to proceed.

"This wall, Laura," I gasped. "It wasn't here before!"

Again, Laura, confused, looked at me as if to say, "Get yourself together—there's no wall!"

At that moment, with me hanging on to the railing for dear life, fifty people waiting behind me, and Laura, in her confusion, wanting to help but not knowing at all what I was going through, an immense voice pealed through the Grand Gallery.

It was a stern, bold male voice that spoke: "How dare you enter this Holy of Holies without permission!" he said. "Who are you to lead these initiates through the gate?"

To this day, I cannot believe I managed to hold on to those rungs in the ladder without being blown right off the stairway and plummeting to my death.

Was it Thoth, "speaking the word" that held the vibrational codes to unlocking the stargate?

I turned back around to see not fifty but hundreds of people filling the chamber, all in white robes, all waiting for me to get past the stairwell and proceed into the chamber.

I could not believe what I was seeing. The entire gallery was filled with souls.

It took every ounce of strength to utter the words: "There is a gate. We must ask for permission to enter."

The energy that rolled through every one of us was palpable—electrifying.

I looked back up at the obstructing wall.

"I am a humble servant of the light," I spoke into the ethers. "We come to honor all who have passed here before us—and to celebrate all that lies beyond.. . ."

Then, unintelligible to my conscious awareness, I muttered some sounds, as if a prayer were being spoken through me. I could not make sense of them and knew they were not of a language I recognized—a phenomenon that repeats itself when I am in ceremony in Egypt.

Apparently, they were the key to opening the gate.

Instantly, the wall I had seen with my inner eye crumbled, and we were free to pass through.

There, in the Ascension Room (for that is what the King's Chamber really is), we brought the music of life through our hearts and souls, and the interdimensional walls of the pyramid played like a galactic organ, sounding the harmonies of timeless journeyers, fusing the dimensions. Joining us in this great chorus of souls and angels were etheric beings of many dimensions, many of whom had appeared at the stairwells, and there were astral forms of the earthly masters, Tibetan Lamas, who know how to travel the electromagnetic energy lines of Gaia as "sound."

To each of the initiating was given time to lie in the granite "sarcophagus," to be propelled to the stars, the no-time, as other priests and priestesses—the pharaohs themselves—had surely done before us.

We experienced sheer magic, as time completely disappeared for us all and we felt the great granite walls undulate like waves of light. For a moment, far from the chaos of the world, we were right there, on the other side of the veil, knowing timelessness—dimensions beyond—far beyond what we have come to know as our earthly "reality."

Once you have such an experience, you know you have broken through to the higher realms and that you have touched greatness.

~

The pyramids at Giza are perfectly aligned to the stars. This we have had elaborated for us in the works of archeo-astrologers like Robert Bauval and his rival, Kate Spence (each claiming ownership of the "wisdom"), who have shown us the maps to some very interesting theories.

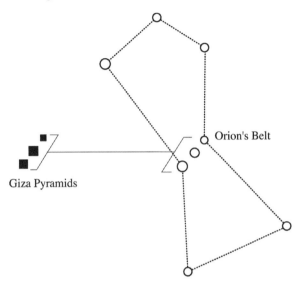

Of these, Bauval is credited with the star correlation theory (which was actually first presented by Victoria Trimble), based on astronomical alignments traced back to the pyramids at about 10,500 BC. The pyramid layout does, in fact, bear remarkable alignment with the stars of Orion's Belt and provides an interesting perspective on the early Egyptians' awareness—perhaps—of their own stellar origins.

This work is well known enough to us all by now, the subject of many a television documentary and books, so that it requires no elaboration.

Of far greater interest are the precise alignments of the primary shafts of the Great Pyramid, gateways of the early pharaohs, during that same time reference (circa 10,500 BC) to the stars of Orion, Sirius, Ursa Minor, and Alpha Draconis.

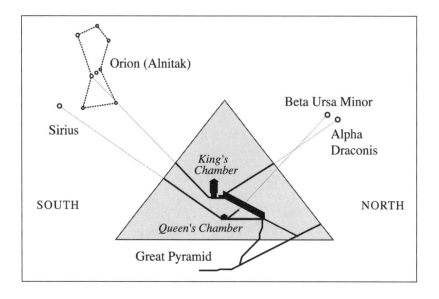

Note, in the drawing, that the King's Chamber aligns perfectly with Alnitak, the first star in the belt of Orion.

At a recent crystal skull conference in Milan, where I was a keynote speaker, I enjoyed a very brief but exceptional opportunity to meditate with the famous Mitchell-Hedges crystal skull. Whether or not the skull is one of the Atlantean skulls, or whether it is a fake, as recent investigations wish to imply, was not my concern and still is not important to me. Whatever its history, this is a magnificent crystal, a fabulous tool for scrying. I was honored to have the possibility to connect with it in person.

For the purposes of this book, the intention of which is to bring to you the right-brained experience beyond the left-brained theories, I asked the skull to illuminate for me the true purpose of the King's Chamber—that I be shown with the mind's eye what the pharaohs' secrets held.

Remarkably, the skull manifested a whir of light images within it. Seconds later, I saw a saucer-like shape appear, which perfectly resembled a flying saucer—right at a point on the forehead of the skull, which corresponds to the third eye on a human skull.

Just above it, a recognizable, cloudy formation took form, which I knew I had seen before in visions. I immediately identified it as the Horsehead Nebula, located near Alnitak, the star associated with the Great Pyramid, in the constellation of Orion, supposedly 1,550 light-years from Earth.

In the excitement of that vision, a journalist snapped three consecutive photos of me scrying with the skull, in which the vision is clearly captured in the photographs. *See Frame 17.*

What I saw in the viewing screen of the Mitchell-Hedges skull is a psychic answer to my question and that is how I present it to you: that beings from Alnitak did assist in the planning of the Great Pyramid, that the pharaohs knew their starseed origins ... and that they were shown the astro-highways of the long road home.

And you? What do you see looking back at you in these images—from the extra-dimensional lens of the world's most renowned crystal skull? *See Frame 18.*

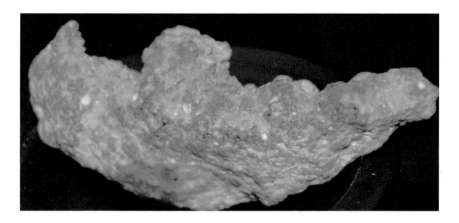

1: The Ship.

2: The Temple of Hatshepsut.

❧ 3: Hathor at Hatshepsut Temple.
❧ 4: Amir with Patricia at the Cafeteria.

❧ 5: Hakim and Patricia on the Balcony.
❧ 6: Karnak at Sunrise

9: Sekhmet Fire.

7: Ptah at the Chapel.

8: Ptah at Abydos.

∾ 10: Private Ceremony
at the Sphinx.

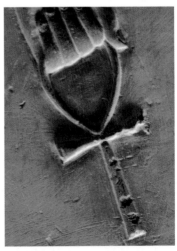

∾ 11: The Key.

∾ 12: Horus in the Hills.

⌇ 13A: Ma'at Appears in the Darkness.

⌇ 13B: Ma'at Defined.

✑ 13C: Ma'at at Abydos.

✑ 14: Isis Alights.

෨ 15: Seshet
with Thoth.

෨ 16A: Thoth
in the Cup.

༁ 16B: The Ibis.

෨ 17: The Horsehead Nebula.

❧ 18: Inside the Skull.

∽ 20A: The Way to the Tunnel.

∽ 20B: Souls in the Duat.

21: The Orb at Osireion.

22: Estrella.

19: The Temple Ear.

23: Shaft Entrance.

24A and B: Into
the Deep.

∾ 13

The Mysterious Osireion

After our time in the Great Pyramid, we flew to Luxor, where the first day was dedicated to the Sekhmet initiations, as recounted earlier on in my story. Building upon these powerful experiences, in which all were opening to the mysteries of Egypt, we left the next morning, traveling again on the police-escorted convoy, for Abydos.

By now my antennae could pick up Amir's energy from a distance, so I was not surprised that he was the very first person I saw when I got off the bus. It was as if he sensed my return would be that very day, although there had been no plan or communication about it. He just seemed to be waiting for me to "come home."

After the heat and the tedium of the long drive, the group was anxious to enter the temple with our guide, Nabel, and with no time to do more than just barely introduce them to Amir, I watched them move past me, eagerly following Nabel up to the courtyard and away.

I stayed back yet again, as I had in every other occasion in Abydos, leaving the group to enjoy the wisdom of our well-versed guide and knowing that time with Amir was far more important to me personally than whatever I would learn from the Egyptologists' rendition as to the "accepted" meanings and interpretations of the gods and their interactions with the pharaoh.

Amir and I were reunited once again.

After ordering the ceremonial tea, and wasting no time on formalities, Amir looked deep into my eyes and said, "You know that the time has come for you to walk in the footsteps of Omm Sety."

He seemed pensive, as if speaking the words themselves were some extraordinary commitment that he had not planned on making.

"Those are pretty big shoes to fill," I said.

Amir looked at me with wide-eyed innocence.

"Omm Sety walked without shoes," he said, looking around, furtively, as if what he was to say were too important for others to hear.

"There are so many secrets here for you to discover," he said, "but you need more time with us . . . much more time."

I understood perfectly that these short visits were no more than teasers for what I was to discover.

". . . and you need to come by yourself," he said, emphatically, "for at least two weeks—at the very least."

I looked around at the poor village and wondered how I could possibly find a decent place to stay.

Amir must have read my mind. He told me there was a foreigner, Kevin, who had a small bed and breakfast and I could stay there. I **would** stay there—it seemed—without question.

"If I had a guide who knew how to open the gates for me, I would come," I said, glancing slyly at Amir, studying his reactions. I knew that he understood I was talking about gates to hidden chambers, but did he realize I was looking for keys to other realms?

"The gates can be opened," he replied, assuredly, "but that guide would need for you to be here for much more time, much more time than this."

"I can come," I stated decisively.

Amir nodded, staring deep into my soul, and said: "Let the gates be open then."

I decided then that within months I would return and stay as long as it took for me to taste the Secret Wisdom laced through the ethers of Abydos. Given my commitments at home, though, "as long as it took" could never be more than two weeks' time.

We sat in quiet recognition of what we had committed to each other, knowing it was important . . . knowing no other words needed to be spoken. Once we finished the tea, I told him I needed to join my group inside the temple and he accompanied me. In the craziness of the tourist frenzy, the people in the group had scattered and were busily exploring and finding their own discoveries within the temple's many magical spaces.

Amir said, "You still have not been in the Osireion," and with that, he guided me through the hypostyle hall toward the passageway that leads to the back stairway—out to the more ancient temple structure. There, I believe, is buried one of the most important keys to our global transition from this time of darkness into the Light.

This magnificent structure is located behind the Temple of Sety I, at a much lower elevation (more than thirty feet below) in the rocky substrata of the sands of the temple grounds. Apparently, it was named the "Osireion" by famed archeologists Margaret

Murray and Flinders Petrie, back in the early part of the twen-
tieth century, when they were excavating the site. A debate as to
the age of this extraordinary building has raged ever since.

Hakim says flatly that the Khemitian tradition places the
Osireion as contemporary to the Great Sphinx: both more than
50,000 years old.

Many orthodox Egyptologists claim it was actually built by
Sety I, a deduction based on not much more than a simple dec-
oration carved on one of the ceilings in the Osireion that bears
his name—a relatively insignificant element on which to determine the origins of such a monumental structure. Considering
the inscription could easily have been added millennia later (perhaps when Sety's construction crew ran into the structure during the building of his temple), I find this simplistic evaluation of
the Osireion's age tenuous, at best.

The only other evidence attesting to Sety's possible construction of the Osireion was, according to Omm Sety, the pharaoh's
name found "on a black granite cramp inserted between two
blocks of a red granite architrave," which was inserted to hold
the two pieces from springing apart. This, too, could clearly have
been executed thousands of years later, and leads even the most
unscholarly explorer to question the soundness of dating the
structure to a far more recent time line.

In her wonderful book *Abydos: Holy City of Ancient Egypt* (co-
authored with Dr. Hanny El Zeini), Omm Sety herself says that
it was "only one of the many restorations to ancient monuments
carried out by Sety," adding that "it is no proof of his contribution to the construction of the building."

Given that nowhere in the story-lines of his temple did Sety
I ever claim to have built the Osireion, a monumental and glo-

rious achievement that would have been the pride of any king, it seems obvious (to me, at least) that we are looking at another Egyptian anomaly.

This truly awe-inspiring structure is so utterly diverse from other temple structures in Egypt, with the exception of the Sphinx and the Valley Temple (which Hakim also pre-dates to ancient time lines of the Khemitians), that it is almost preposterous that the "experts" dismiss it as being contemporary to the New Kingdom temple above it.

Read any commercial guidebook to Egypt and you will see the Temple of Sety I described as a "unique building site," from the point of view of its "L-shaped" design. Whereas other contemporary temples were built in a classical, rectangular design, the temple seems to have changed course mid-build, which some scholars believe is the result of Sety's building team running into the Osireion during construction, forcing a dramatic architectural alteration to the classic blueprint.

Omm Sety's writings reveal very little about the Osireion and yet she knew and celebrated almost every inch of the Temple of Sety I. Perhaps the more ancient structure had been a mere backdrop to the more artistic temple above it, where she vividly recalled that compelling lifetime as a young priestess, and how she had been taken to the temple to live her devotion to the gods—devotion interrupted by her passionate love affair with the pharaoh.

Surely, had they been contemporary structures, the visionary Omm Sety would have had much more to tell of the Osireion as well!

It appears there is far more to the story.

As magnificent as Sety's temple is, with its majestic hypostyle halls and breathtakingly sculpted chambers and outer walls, it was the Osireion that drew me back, energetically, then. Even now, at this writing, as I sit in the Cafeteria, adding these pieces to the ever-growing puzzle . . . it is the mystery of the great Osireion that calls out, to be brought into the light of Khepre—the Awakening.

I knew there were powerful messages to be retrieved there, inside the courtyard and inner sanctum of the Osireion, and I was eager to explore it for myself—to discover my own truths from the obscurity of its shrouded halls.

Amir led me to the stairway through the back of the temple, clearly not the original entrance to the megalithic site, and we walked down a rough passageway across rocky sandstone, to an observation point, from the southern side, where a rickety stairway tempts the visitor down near (but not **into**) the outer "courtyard." Entry into the courtyard as well as the inner rooms is strictly forbidden, and there are police guards stationed everywhere, making sure the visitor understands that means **you.**

That would be for another visit, soon, when time would not be an issue, and when the doors would open to permit me entry, as they have on so many other occasions in my life—when it has been the **right** time.

At that moment of early initiations into the Egyptian mysteries, I was still blinded to the secrets held within the megalithic structure, not yet ready, perhaps, to receive the information that would come later . . . and I was distracted by the putrid, slimy waters that covered more than two feet of the outer grounds and denied access to the inner sanctum.

I had read in Omm Sety's books that the waters of the Osireion were the holiest of waters and that still then, during her lifetime, miracles would be performed through their healing properties. But now, it seemed, so short a time from her death, it appeared only filth and the foulest smells remained of that blessed state.

These were appearances I would dispel later, when spirit would guide me in, past judgment, past fear . . . past the surface and into a deeper understanding of the memory water holds.

In that first encounter with the Osireion, however, something huge was stirred within me. I looked down upon it from the improvised stairway, fascinated—drawn in—knowing it, as if I had lived it.

In that short time of observation, Amir walked me around to a sealed-off location, where I could look down into an outer chamber, believed to have been the chamber of embalming—a chapel to Anubis. I knew it was more than that.

I could see into the space enough to recognize a tunnel connected to this chamber and I wondered where it led. Amir said simply that it was "one of the secrets he wanted me to explore," and we left it at that . . . knowing there was no time then to delve further into it.

After completing the tour with my group of spirit seekers, I returned home enthralled—almost obsessed—with the Osireion and the profound possibilities that lay within its mysterious shroud. It seemed to be holding a veil over what I believed I would discover was an entry point to the Halls of Amenti, where the thirteenth crystal skull could be held in the light waves of some incredibly advanced Sirian technology, and where there could very likely be underwater rivers and roads leading through the Egypt we have yet to rediscover—all the way through to Agharta and the hidden paradise of Shamballah.

As I explored photographs of the Osireion, the proverbial light bulb went off in my head, as I almost immediately recognized its similarity to the background building in Leonardo Da Vinci's famous work *The Last Supper.*

I searched for an image of his masterpiece to find that, to my amazement, the building in which the scene of the supper is portrayed is so absolutely similar to the perspective of the Osireion in my photo that it remains difficult to dismiss it as mere coincidence.

Indeed, if you place the dining table of the Supper at the second horizontal line in the floor of the Osireion (where the stones are cut) you find that the number of columns depicted is equal to the number in the painting and the position of Jesus is right in line with the indentation where it has been suggested the tomb of Osiris was situated. The mysterious marble in front of the table, before the Christ, is perfectly proportionate to the stairway in the Osireion, which Egyptologists believe may have been used for initiatory rituals.

Clearly, the portal behind Christ finds its counterpart in the

opening in the Osireion courtyard that leads into the tunnel, which represents the journey through the Duat.

Following *The Da Vinci Code* hysteria, there has been untold speculation over the significance and hidden meanings in the masterpieces. Much of this has been primarily focused on the question (proposed in Dan Brown's book) of whether it is Mary Magdalene, and not St. John, seated at the right hand of Jesus.

As to the artistic structure of the painting itself, much has been written about Da Vinci's use of Divine Proportion, derived from the golden mean ratio, which forms the basis of our study of sacred geometry. It is the measure used from the most ancient of times: the Great Pyramid itself; the Greek Parthenon; Da Vinci's masterpiece.

Nothing that I have ever come across, however, describes the fascinating parallels between the painting of the actual building that contains the scene of Christ and his disciples and the image of the Osireion, photographed from inside the courtyard, just outside the doorway that leads into the so-called sarcophagus room.

Da Vinci has aligned all the elements in Divine Proportion, nestling his subjects, twelve-around-one, inside a structure that mirrors the courtyard of the Osireion. The trained eye notes immediately that the disciples are grouped in four groupings of three, reflecting the sacred geometry of the Great Pyramid. It is as if the building or structure of Da Vinci's painting itself contains, by far, more secret coding than the figures at the great feast: the twelve apostles around the One—the Christ.

What is his secret?

Could *The Last Supper* just possibly be Da Vinci's hidden map to the Portal of Nephthys (the goddess of the enclosure), which held the crystal skulls within its frame? It is so unquestionably similar to the Osireion, I often wonder why this has never been investigated by art historians and philosophers intent upon revealing the hidden meanings and codes in the great works.

Years of working with crystals of every shape and form have brought me into perpetual resonance with these living beings, and I have learned, over these wondrous years, just what incredible vehicles of spiritual transportation and vision they truly are.

Searching to find the answer to the question of the Osireion's true purpose, I meditated with my favorite quartz crystal sphere, one that I am most successful with when scrying. I asked to be shown if there was, indeed, a portal there—where the greatest secrets lay hidden. As I began to see into the cloudy window of the sphere, opening upon other dimensions, I saw what resembles the right side of the walls of the Osireion appear in the exact center of the crystalline structure. Remarkably, the image has remained inexplicably imprinted in the sphere, as if some divine artist, gifting me with otherworldly "proof," has sculpted the image into the quartz.

I grabbed my camera and took this amazing shot of the image, which seems to be permanently engraved within the center of the magical sphere.

Gaze into the image and you clearly see the right wall of columns and doorways of the Osireion. Are you able to make out that on the left side there appears to be a figure in white?

There is the figure of Osiris, in his mummified form, pointing the way. Through the magical lens of the crystal sphere, I was being shown the answer.

"... The doorway is there," it seemed to be telling me. "You just need to find your way home...."

∾ 14

Pure Magic

Having considered how this twelve-around-one concept mirrors the Crystal Skull Committee, I became even more intrigued with the powers of the Osireion and knew I couldn't wait much longer to enter its magical spaces and secret tunnels to other worlds. A very few months later, after the group journey, I hurried back to my beloved Abydos. I had made an appointment with what was clearly my destiny to get inside the monument alone and to feel it firsthand, uninterrupted and unhurried.

Amir had arranged everything with Kevin, who has become a dear friend and a sort of "haven" for me in Abydos. He still hosts me during my many visits in his comfortable little B&B, which is quietly becoming known to those seekers, like me, who are drawn to the place for more than just the short visit a day's journey can provide.

An icon of the village, Kevin is a brilliant guy with an in-depth knowledge of Egyptian history and mythology. We have filled many an evening contemplating the mysteries of Egypt: me, with my metaphysical sense of it all; Kevin, with his utterly masterful knowledge of Egyptian history and archeology.

Soon after settling in at Kevin's, I rejoined Amir in the Cafeteria, waiting for the convoy of tourists to leave before returning to the temple.

As always, Abydos welcomed me with open arms. By now, the locals knew me, and they all seemed genuinely pleased to see me back. It all eerily reflected a sense of having been there before—a sense of truly belonging to the place.

I sat with Amir, drinking our ritual tea, preparing for the journey of discovery I knew had begun long, long ago—so many moons before that very first time I had come to Abydos.

With time enough, finally, to investigate every inch of the Temple of Sety I, as well as the Osireion, I decided to take my sweet time exploring, dedicating each day to one of the inner chapels. Amir would diligently accompany me into the temple every morning and guard the space around me, creating a protective shield that no one dared enter.

Everywhere, Seshet's plume seemed to write the records on the walls of my mind.

The second morning of that particular sojourn, as I sat in the Chapel of Isis, my eyes were drawn to a remarkably beautiful carving on the wall, one that seemed to leap out at me, asking to be noticed.

It was a most perfect, beautiful depiction of Sety offering the gods a small effigy of the goddess Ma'at, which sat in his palm, and this same Ma'at figure was offering, from her palm, yet another, smaller sized Ma'at. This smaller figure of Ma'at held out another, smaller Ma'at and finally that one, the third Ma'at figure, held out to the gods a depiction of herself that was so utterly miniscule you could just barely make out the fine features, perfectly etched in meticulous detail.

I remember looking at it, thinking that, of all the magnificent artwork I had seen in the temple, nothing had impacted me quite like this, especially since Ma'at held such importance to my own experience and those early discoveries, after the regression.

I left the chamber and went on to explore other aspects of the temple and, after much "lost" time drifting in the beauty of those hallowed halls, I left to join Amir and Kevin for a bite of lunch at the Cafeteria.

Later that evening, Kevin was sharing some of his keen observations about the temple art and history.

Out of the blue, he said: "There is a most exquisite depiction of Sety offering Ma'at out to the gods, and then Ma'at offering herself as well—again and again.. . ."

I was amazed that out of all the possible images and scenes depicted in the temple, he would choose to describe what I had been focused on all morning: Ma'at then offering Ma'at, offering Ma'at and Ma'at again. It was such serendipity!

"I saw it once," he added, "but I have never been able to find it again."

He looked at me quizzically, and added: "It is hiding somewhere in there."

I told him I had **just** seen it—and described how it had almost "jumped out at me" from the wall.

Kevin asked me where I had seen it and I told him it was in the second chapel, for sure. He said he was sure he had seen it on the wall of the second hypostyle hall, but when he looked again it wasn't there.

I corrected him—I was absolutely sure I had just seen it in the Chapel of Isis.

The next morning I couldn't wait to get in and take another look at the breathtaking carving ... but it wasn't there. I was certain it had been there—I had just spent hours gazing at it! Yet, there was nothing of the kind on the walls in that chapel—where I was sure I had seen it leap from the wall into my conscious mindstream.

Mystified, I retraced my steps, conceding that I might have been mistaken, but certain I hadn't. It had been there, inside the chapel, for **sure.**

Kevin and I entered into a relatively animated conversation about it. He kept insisting that sometimes the temple "hides" things, whereas I was realizing that what was, in effect, happening was that we were somehow seeing beyond the third dimension ... where this very powerful image held resonance.

The next morning, over coffee with Amir, I asked him if he had ever seen this carving of Sety offering Ma'at, who then offers herself over and over again, to the gods. It doesn't even make sense, thinking it through, that a quintessential god such as Ma'at would be depicted offering herself to other gods.. . .

"Yes," he said, pensively, as if trying to recall it.

"Do you know where it is?" I asked, eager to see it again.

Amir said, "I have seen it only once—a few years ago ... but I have never seen it again after that."

I asked him if he thought it odd that he couldn't retrace his steps to find the image again and he echoed Kevin's comment about how the temple "hides things."

I thought this was an odd observation, coming from two people who had full access to explore the temple anytime they wanted, at will. Surely, I thought, someone who had "misplaced" an ancient wall carving would have searched for it diligently—and then, unsuccessful, would have had to question his own sanity.

I wanted to be absolutely sure my mind was not playing tricks on me and so I spent the next two days poring over every relief in the temple, in search of the curious image. I walked through the entire complex at least four times, studying every wall, searching every space . . . but the splendid relief of Sety's offering of Ma'at with its fractal-like representations of Ma'at in diminishing forms, the offerings of her own effigy, was absolutely nowhere to be found.

It was as if the first depiction, Sety offering Ma'at, represented the third dimension; Ma'at offering the smaller Ma'at represented the fourth; that image, with yet a smaller Ma'at in her hand—the fifth; and finally the miniscule Ma'at, offered yet again, seemed to speak of a sixth-dimensional representation of the goddess.

The sixth dimension, of course, is where the Sirians of the ascended star (the star of Osiris) Satais reside.

With Amir to translate for me, I queried the guards at the temple. If this carving existed in this temple, by the gods I was determined I would find it. One guard, who had worked there for more than thirty years, said he had seen the image the year before, for the first time, and now he couldn't remember where it was. He went into the temple to search for it, convinced he could remember and then show it to me . . . but the next day he told us, perplexed, that he couldn't find it, either.

Kevin said two other people had seen it and they, too, were mystified when they could not find it again.

Here was proof that the temple itself was giving us all a taste of what lies beyond the illusion and proof, too, that reality, at Abydos at least, was far more than what we understand it to be

... and that just because something is "written in stone" may not necessarily mean it is fact.

Sety's temple, his magnificent homage to the gods and legacy to humankind, was all but telling me: "I am the portal between the Kingdoms of Light."

And I could hear it speak to me, pillar to pillar, just a whisper ... but I could hear it speak to my heart of magical things.

Perhaps that is why one finds the carving of a human ear on the wall that leads up the stairway and out to the Osireion. *See Frame 19.*

The temple lives: it listens, just as it speaks.

It is the ear of the temple, itself a living entity, listening to all who enter, awaiting the Adept who has attuned to the word of the Creator God to speak the names of Osiris. There in the hall where the name of each gate is recorded in the walls, the ear of the temple is also carved.

Is the ear waiting to hear from the Spirit Master who will have "gathered together of 'them' by name," unlocking the portal, as I believe is intimated in the Book of Gates?

As for the Ma'at mystery, the only plausible explanation (other than accepting that we were all utterly out of our minds) was that this image of hauntingly profound significance was indeed appearing to us from another dimension, beyond the reality of those three-dimensional walls at Abydos that seem to be just barely holding form in the density of our rapidly shifting physical reality.

Those of us who had seen the carving had been privileged to just a glimpse beyond the veil that separates us from the higher dimensions ... and then it disappeared—the drape falling again, like some great theatrical curtain call.

It had been important enough for us all to notice it . . . to delight in it and to search, over and over again—to find it.

It had been powerful enough to challenge even the most skeptical Egyptian guards as to their perception of truth and reality.

But no amount of searching for "Ma'at to the sixth dimension" has made her reappear to any one of us.

Amir and I came back to this strange phenomenon over and over again, throughout my stay. He told me that the villagers were actually quite terrified of the temple. They would hear strange sounds coming from it at night, and often see lights emanating from the skylights that formed part of the roof structure.

He recounted the story of a guard who fell asleep inside the temple grounds, somewhere out of sight of his fellow guards. At the end of the day, when it was time to close the temple and lock up the grounds, nobody realized the man was still inside. The guards went about their normal procedures and, at closing time, unknowingly closed the sleeping sentinel inside, with no exit.

Locked inside the temple in pitch darkness, the terrified man awakened from his late siesta to the sight of gods and goddesses "stepping off the walls," as he later described to the village people, and then conversing and moving around through the temple!

The hysterical man told how he raced to the main entrance gate in sheer delirium, screaming for someone to come and get him out. By the time help came, Amir said, he had gone insane, overwrought from the terror of his visions. Apparently, he was never the same again.

The local people dismissed his experience as the ranting of a crazed man, but not Amir. He said he knew there was truth in the man's wild story—but never told me why until days later, after I had convinced him to help me arrange to be alone in the temple, in the sweet silence of night.

After the experience of the disappearing Ma'at carving, reinforced by the story of the guard's visions in the darkened temple, I knew I needed to spend time alone there, in the dark, to meet the gods and spirits—on their terms.

I asked Amir if it could be arranged.

Of course it could not, legally. To be inside an Egyptian temple after closing, without permission, would be considered a criminal activity and would surely land both Amir and me in jail . . . were we to be found out.

For that reason, I cannot explain how it was arranged for me to do just that: another illegal entry into one of Egypt's most sacred portals. But I can tell you what happened there.

I was to enter, at closing time, back into the sacred Chapel of Isis, one of the most powerful locations inside the temple, where one can feel the energy lines intersecting outside the chapel entranceway. There I would wait until the temple was cleared and the lights were turned off.

The guards would pretend they didn't know I was still inside and they would basically lock me in, as they had unknowingly done to the guard years earlier.

I was told I would have to come out after one hour, whereupon I would be escorted back to the Cafeteria, as best as possible, concealed in the night, and then accompanied back to Kevin's.

Amir was clearly concerned and warned me that he had misgivings about my being alone in the temple in the night hours. He felt the same madness that befell the guard could envelop me as well. I assured him that I was not fearful of spirits. I knew that the temple was sacred space and I knew what to do there, just like Omm Sety. I felt at home, loved and protected within those holy walls, a place I do truly believe I have walked before.

Reluctant and with great trepidation, Amir agreed.

Admittedly, it was a bit eerie when I heard the guards at the front gate turn the key, once, twice, again and again—until finally the bolt was locked. The lights were turned off; the temple fell silent.

I was locked inside, all alone, in the Temple of Sety I.

I lit incense and laid a blanket across the cold marble pavement in the Isis chamber, invoking the goddess Isis to surround me in her love and light. It was as if her great wings encircled me, holding me in her protective embrace, like an infant in the womb.

As I lay there, meditating, I opened my eyes to gaze upon the breathtakingly beautiful images on the walls. Despite the lack of artificial light, there was a sunroof in the chamber and the light of Ra still shone into the room, so that everything was still illuminated. As the sun began to set, however, shadows cast upon the walls caused the images to change, reflecting different angles and forms, and I imagined how perhaps the moonlight shining into the temple had fooled the guard into believing the images were moving.

I soon discovered that was not the case and that what the guard had reported he had most likely really **seen.**

Having lost all sense of time, I fell into a deep state of altered consciousness, enveloped in waves of incredible spirit light and powerful, very powerful sensations of transverse energy waves crossing through vortices within the temple. I could hear the voices of the gods . . . and the temple itself, a living deity, played its own music.

I lay there, in bliss, beyond any other experience but surrender—the logical mind silenced, my heart boundless in the wonder of all that was coming into being.

It is an experience I find very difficult to share, to put into words...that it might be misconstrued or in any way dismissed as fantasy, like it had been for the guard who tried to tell his similar story. Yet, I am willing to take that risk now, so that others can know what magic is found in Abydos and so that they may find their way there.

At some indefinable point in this magical time of initiation, something compelled me to sit up. I pulled myself out of the state of deep meditation (or at least I believed I had) and sat upright, so that I was looking out upon the hypostyle hall outside of the chamber.

From the warmth of the nest I had found enfolded in the wings of Isis, I was now looking out at the dark, forbidding hall with its huge pillars and passageways to dark chambers.

An enormous wave of coldness—that psychic freeze—washed through me.

As I peered into the darkness, I began to see light forms gathering at the back of the hall, something like the flickering of candles. I wondered if someone else had entered the temple, perhaps someone sent in to guard me. I looked again, trying to get a better focus, to find that walking toward me was a procession of ancient Egyptian priests.

Their heads were shaved and they were unadorned, dressed in tunics of pure white linen. The priest in the front of the procession carried a basket of fruit and other offerings, and he was heading directly toward me.

All I can remember of my reactions to this amazing vision is that I believed I was in the way of their ceremonial homage to Isis. I tried to move out of her chamber, but I could not move my body in any way. I was in another dimension, disconnected from the physical realm.

I stared in astonishment into the hall with its ghostly apparitions. There were six priests in the scene, slowly moving toward me, toward the Chamber of Isis, goddess of love and light. And there I was, in the middle, blocking their access to her.

As I sat there, immobilized, I saw the High Priest, perhaps Sety himself, emerge from the back of the procession, behind the others. He was dressed in an elaborate gown, bejeweled with amulets and gold, and he wore the traditional uraeus crown of gods and pharaohs. He was walking to the left side of the procession, moving closer to me.

He reached the point where the first priest had stopped, about six feet before the entrance to the chamber, and started to come toward me, while the priest, kneeling on one knee, placing the offering tray on the ground.

Just then, as the High Priest looked right into me, rays of light shining like lasers from his eyes to mine, a voice called out in the darkness.

"Hello?" A man's voice ricocheted through the temple.

I had no idea where this voice was coming from and simply didn't care.

I was silent, still immersed in what was unfolding, observing the incredible spirits before me, while receiving the enormous hit of light from the eyes of the High Priest, right into my soul. It was reverberating through my head, racing through my spinal column.

"Hello, hello?" The intrusive call came again, insistent, from the outer halls of the temple.

This was enough to jerk me back into the world of the physical. Regrettably, the priests and the magic of that incredible moment dissipated, as their images disintegrated into the ethers and I crashed back into the reality of where I was—in the temple, in the dark, in Abydos.

I forced myself to stand up, and then staggered out into the hypostyle hall.

"Yes?" I called out in the darkness, like someone who had been jolted out of a beautiful dream from deep sleep.

The voice replied: "Please, madam, we must go quickly!"

I saw no one. Only the voice, bouncing from wall to wall, convinced me that someone human had entered the dark space of the unlit temple.

Still reeling from what I had known in the magic of Isis's wings, I gathered up my blanket and the few spiritual tools I had brought with me and made my way, staggering, to the doorway. There stood the guard who had been instrumental in the arrangements, looking more than just a little frightened. He didn't want to step foot in the temple and was clearly uncomfortable even being near the entrance in the hours of the night—and no doubt, he thought I was crazy for attempting it.

He told me a villager had reported to the police that someone was inside the temple and that we had just seconds to get me out of harm's way before they came to investigate.

Like a scene from *Casablanca*, I was escorted to safety, back to the Cafeteria, where I could barely make out the moonlit faces of some of the local men in the village, who were smoking their shisha pipes in the cool of the night. They looked at me curiously, not knowing what to make of a woman out at night. This clearly never happens in their ancient village.

As always, Amir was there, waiting for me to return.

"What happened?" he asked, clearly upset.

Still dazed, I struggled to answer him, but I still had not completely returned to full body awareness.

"You were supposed to be there for one hour," he said. "Why didn't you come out—Patricia—I was so worried about you!"

I could see that he was genuinely distressed.

I looked at him quizzically, realizing I had no idea of the time … and a very distorted sense of space.

"Why, Amir?" I asked, confused. "What time is it?"

Amir told me it was past nine, which meant I had been in the temple for more than five hours!

I was flabbergasted. What had seemed like just a blush of time had actually been more than five hours?

Smoking cigarette after cigarette, Amir tried to calm himself, while waiting for me to describe what had happened inside. I wanted to share it with him, but it was so powerful that it simply defied words.

I needed time to be with the experience … to explore the meaning of what had happened there. And more—I felt that I was, in many ways, still in it—still resonating to the frequencies of the priesthood, with just one toe dipped into the reality of the dense three-dimensional world, and the rest of me adrift in another time and space.

I promised Amir I would tell him about it later, once I had had a chance to work through it all.

I went back to Kevin's place and lay down, thoughts of the ceremony and ancient priests racing around in my head, and there I lay—sleepless, as I gazed at the ceiling until dawn.

The next morning, I went to meet Amir as soon as he opened

up the Cafeteria in early morning. I couldn't wait to tell him what had occurred inside and I knew he couldn't wait to hear.

As I recounted my experience of the priests, he interrupted me. Very pointedly, he asked me: "How were they dressed?"

I told him they were dressed in simple white linen tunics and then I continued the story of what had unfolded.

Again, Amir interrupted.

"How many were there?" he asked.

"Six," I answered, surprised that he was focusing on these details and not actually following my story.

He said, "Six?" as if this meant something to him. He seemed almost disappointed, as if "six" were not the right answer to whatever he was searching for.

"There were six priests, Amir," I answered agitatedly, "and one High Priest, who came at the end of the procession."

At the mention of the High Priest, Amir became excited. He told me a story, which he has given me permission to retell here, about a very respectable man in the village, whose house sits on sacred ground, right next to the temple.

Amir described the man as a "simple" person, a devout Moslem, and one who is certainly not up to inventing stories of the mystical variety.

It seems that years earlier, this man was visited in his sleep by the same group of priests: six in simple white tunics, and a High Priest, whom Amir says the man described almost exactly as I had. These apparitions began to surface in his dreams, causing untold stress and fear. They were very threatening experiences, wherein the priests were telling him to get off the land and clear the space. Apparently, from what he told Amir, they were telling him that the garbage and sewage from his home were seeping into the temple inner courts and this could not be allowed. They were intent upon scaring him away: off the temple land; out of their most sacred space.

These visitations went on for months, even in awakened states, always frightening the poor man to death, but he had nowhere else to go. He asked them to forgive him, but he had a family and they had no other way but to stay there. It seems the tormented dreams and visions eventually stopped after that, but to Amir he has told the story over and over again, with precision, and each time, Amir says, he can see that the man is still filled with terror.

"When you told me it was six priests and a High Priest," Amir said, "I knew it was the same spirits that this man talked about."

I nodded in agreement.

"No one else has ever seen them," he mused.

". . . But there they remain," I replied, touched, almost tormented, by the idea that priestly spirits still haunt the halls of holy Abydos, dedicated to keeping its integrity intact from their side of the veil.

We looked at each other, knowing it was a profound moment, silently recognizing how my walking in "Omm Sety's footsteps" had revealed to us both that the mysteries of Abydos and its priesthood were still very much **alive.**

When the time finally arrived for me to physically enter the ancient Osireion, I cast off any information I had acquired about the history, archaeology, and the actual purpose of the mysterious structure and decided that what I had discovered through my own metaphysical "channels" was the best guide I would have to finding my own answers—right there, at the source.

My first approach to the Osireion would be via the mysterious tunnel—ignoring the fact of its being locked, guarded, and absolutely off-limits. It just made sense (to me, at least!) that a search for a multidimensional passageway into some indefinable otherworld would begin by walking through this ancient corridor, looking for clues and tuned in to receive its altered vibrations.

There was basically only one way to access this space: across the sands (a substantial distance from the northern wall of the temple)...right past the guards and through a locked gate.

As usual, it was dangerous, even though the tipping ceremonies were being handled for me, behind the scenes. Getting caught could have meant—once again—time in an Egyptian jail.

I went anyway.

Despite the strictest police regulations, forbidding entry and prohibiting even walking out there in the desert, things were arranged for me, so that I could test my mettle yet again. No doubt, by then word was out that I was the same crazy woman who had braved the temple alone at night. I got the very distinct impression that some of the guards were at the very least fascinated, and that, in a certain sense, I had gained their respect.

I slid down the huge sand dune and almost fell up against the metal gate that sealed off the tunnel, where I was met by a very nervous gatekeeper. He turned the key, opened the iron door just enough for me to pass through, and then vanished. *See Frame 20.*

I entered the space a wary explorer, asking permission to approach, and reciting the mantra that I have created from the phonetic interpretation of the names of the twelve gates of the Book of the Dead. For all I knew, there could easily have been some determinedly unwelcoming beings hovering, so I was sure to surround myself in the golden white light of the angelic realms. And, of course, my Sirian guides were right there, by my side.

Walking slowly through the dark tunnel, I saw the strange images that had been painted on the walls: images like nothing I had ever seen before. They had a darkness to them that I had never come across before in Egyptian hieroglyphs—at times they were downright macabre. In fact, what I was seeing there was the depiction of the journey through the underworld, hell itself, in all its frightening allegory.

The drawings were rough and unfinished, but nonetheless they painted a picture of the terrifying potential suffering of the soul as it makes its way through the twelve gates: souls with their hearts cut out, others burned, yet others immersed in huge cauldrons of boiling water. *See Frame 21.*

Finally, at the end of this nightmarish journey through the gates, a great scarab is shown coming into the light, representative of the embodiment of Dawn: Hakim's "Khepre." It is the soul's illumination, the hour of arrival—ascension from the earthly planes.

Who, I wondered, were these unfinished images intended for? What ancient authority passed here, and for what reason?

Crawling out of the darkness into the bright light of day, I couldn't help but make the association between my own emergence, from the darkness of that passageway to the bright daylight of Abydos, and that of the beetle, who had greeted me, ever so briefly, at the Temple of Hatshepsut.

Walking this tunnel, living it in those moments, I truly got the sense of how it might be—passing through the dimensions—where the soul is confronted with so much shadow, before passing into light.

Soon after I returned, Amir greeted me with the news that he had arranged for me to spend private time in the grounds of the Osireion and actually enter into the sarcophagus room, so named because it was believed to be the place where the sarcophagus of Osiris had once been.

The murky, foul water was knee deep and I had to submerge my feet and lower legs in what can be described only as a cesspool of pollution, waste, and slime—but clearly I had to raise my consciousness to understand that the water is **sacred.** *See Frame 22.*

As we have been shown, with such eloquence, from the experiments of the noted Dr. Masaru Emoto, every molecule holds the memory of its purest state, always attempting to return to its perfected form, just as it holds the memory of all that passes through it, all that lives within it, and all that has ever been reflected through it.

It is the essence of life on Earth as it is in the Cosmos.

It was necessary to override the repulsion of its appearance and celebrate the higher vibration and intention of these primal waters and this, of itself, was a most important aspect of the initiation.

I would enter, with Amir, and with the skull.

A guardian to thirteen beautiful crystal skulls, I always travel with one of the most magnificent ones, a skull gifted to me by Kayum, a Mayan shaman of the Lacandón tribe, during a ceremony with one of my groups in Palenque, Mexico. In that life-altering moment, I was taken by complete surprise when he unexpectedly removed his headband, **his soul,** and tied it around my head and then bent down to the altar we had created, and handed me the skull: a passing of the guards. He told me months after that he had seen in a vision that I would come—and that the skull was meant to be with me.

Later, one of the people in the group told me that she had heard Kayum say that the skull, whom he called *Estrella* (which means "star" in Spanish), was from **Egypt.**

When I first brought the skull back from Mexico, it spoke to me—asking to be taken to "holy water." At the time, I didn't make the association with the holy water of the Osireion. The first place that came to mind then was the Chalice Well in Glastonbury, England.

I left for England shortly afterward, to bring the skull to the fountain at the Chalice Well, where I placed it in the flow of sacred waters. The skull, formed not of clear quartz but of a denser mineral, faded into the background of the fountain, which appeared rust-colored due to the iron in the water.

My niece, Dana, who had been photographing the skull in the fountain, suddenly called out to me to take a look at the camera.

When we checked the frames, we were both shocked to see a picture of the skull manifesting human form! *See Frame 23.*

The image was captured with a Canon digital camera and has not been retouched in any way other than having been cropped from its original size.

After that event in England, I began having a recurring dream of the skull inside the Osireion and I realized that I was being told, on some level, to bring Estrella to Abydos and to include her in any rituals I would perform there.

One of the most important of the initiatory events of my lifetime was that moment of entering the Osireion's murky waters, which were over knee deep at the time of my entrance there. Ironically, I had to place the crystal skull into the unclean waters for purification, always remembering that the waters of the Osireion are holy and that they hold the memory of all that has flowed through those sacred halls.

This was not an easy task, as the water was deep and the skull could easily have fallen out of reach, into the slimy bottom, so I had to hold on to Estrella, almost plunging myself into the water to my elbows, while slipping into an altered state of consciousness.

My physical sight clouded over, as it does when I begin to "see," and the skull began to speak:

> Beneath these waters lies a secret that you are invited to bring back to the world. Peer into the well, center yourself in humility, and fear not. You are surrounded in the golden white light of Osiris, Master of the light realms of Sirius.
>
> Of the thirteen crystal skulls of Atlantis, which we have described to you as the "Skull Committee," the Master lies in the deep earth below this Temple: the burial place of the Osirian effigy—the gateway to the Halls of Amenti.
>
> It is the thirteenth of those crystal skulls that were gifted to humankind during the time of Atlantis that lies buried here, its etheric blueprint contained within a protective shield, where also is found the DNA of the Sirian Master, Osiris.
>
> Look deep, starseed, deeper than you have ever looked before.
>
> Guided by the Councils of Sirian Light, you have been asked here to unveil the secrets and discover the true road to Amenti. You will have been initiated when you have brought our experience to the Mayalands—where preparations are being made to reunite the Atlantean skulls.
>
> You will be challenged, obstructed, and deterred. It is not new to you; however, this will be your greatest challenge.

*This is the way of the Spirit Warrior. You move forward, egoless,
in service to the All.*

*Always remember, starseed, that your path is illuminated and
you know how to shield yourself from the dark force just as you know
when to shine the light of truth into the shadows.*[8]

Shared with Amir, the experience inside the Osireion, with
Estrella, brought up a storm of emotion, stirring the waters within
and around us, as we made our way closer to the truth that shimmered through the stillness of the unseen currents.

Soon after, I was gifted with yet another Osireion reference from
the crop circles in England. It was shortly after my entry into
the magnificent structure with Amir, that extraordinary experience of initiation and discovery. I woke up on June 29 of that
year to the news that the most unbelievable crop formation had
appeared in the West Kennet Long Barrow, at Avebury in Wiltshire, England.

I stared at the image of this enormous configuration in utter
disbelief. Uncannily, so soon after my return from Abydos, the
Osireion had reappeared, now as an intergalactic message laid
down in the crop fields of sacred England, showing itself to me
in all its magical splendor. It was calling me into its vortex, confirming, guiding . . . pulling me in: showing me the way to
Amenti.

From the great granite pillars of its mighty structure at Abydos, through the imagination of Da Vinci, the Pythagoreans . . .

---

[8] Martine Vallée, ed., *The Great Shift* (San Francisco: Red Wheel/Weiser, LLC, 2009).

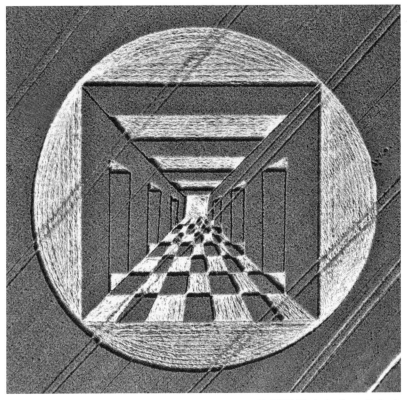

© 2007 *Photo by Lucy Pringle*

and now re-forming itself as the conscious imprint of extra-dimensional beings—the Sirians themselves—I have been shown the way through the gates of immortality, beyond the veils.

And I have been blessed, beyond measure, to have known the spirit beings who guard this incredibly sacred world—the port of entry for the ships of ancient souls.

∾ 15

Entering the Shaft of Osiris

I have found a shaft,

going twenty-nine meters vertically down into the ground,

exactly halfway between the Khefren Pyramid and the Sphinx.

At the bottom, which was filled with water,

we have found a burial chamber with four pillars.

In the middle is a large granite sarcophagus

which I expect to be the grave of Osiris, the god . . .

— Zahi Hawass, *Extra Bladet* newspaper
    Copenhagen, January 31, 1999

Living life as a modern-day, female Indiana Jones is magnificent . . . I admit it. I celebrate all the magic that comes into my life as the fruit of how I choose to walk my path—a glittering trail of stardust strewn just ahead of every step, lighting my way. It is a journey filled with every kind of challenge and adventure: at times, extraordinarily difficult and fraught with danger; at others, silent and still, in the Zen of just being.

It has always been illuminated by some pretty extraordinary people, who have shared in the blessings of many a mystical epiphany.

As you will have understood, from reading these pages or the works that came before them, this remarkable and timeless journey is facilitated by a host of spirit beings as well. Most specifically, it seems to be my Sirian guides who oversee the unfolding events that need to occur in order for me to find my way to the secret doorways and portals, overcoming obstacles and the obstruction of those who would deter me from unveiling a secret or two of our immeasurable power and our immortality.

Undoubtedly, the greatest gift of life is learning that we do not die . . . that we live on, forever, in the ever-evolving forms of our spirit-manifesting-consciousness.

Like the pharaohs, who left so many clues of how they passed from the density of our world to take their place among the stars . . . like beings of other realms, existing in various shades of light body . . . our true path of discovery is the one that leads us through the darkness, beyond the veil, and through the gates of our own glorious eternal life.

My pursuit of understanding how it all knits together has led me to many a mystery, many challenges . . . and I am certain countless others await me, in this dance of life unfolding. Mine is a thirst to discover the secrets of the ages and to share their wisdom with the world, and this I will continue to do as long as I have a breath to breathe . . . until the end of my days.

Effortlessly, the right people, places, and times simply manifest from the most unexpected and unplanned events of my very serendipitous life and I am perennially shown the entranceways to many a "forbidden" temple, sacred site, and no-access zone. From the turning of the keys, to the passing through the stargates, I never cease to be amazed at the wonder of such celestial maneuverings.

Just recently, as I have been drawing these pages to a close, I was given not one, but two opportunities to explore and enter that archeological enigma that Zahi Hawass refers to as the "shaft to the tomb of Osiris," which descends from the midpoint of the Giza Plateau (between the Pyramid of Khefre and the Great Sphinx) straight down to a staggering depth of thirty-three meters (greater than the height of a twelve-story building!), deep into the below of Giza.

From what Zahi Hawass says about the shaft, you get the immediate sense that this is surely an epicentral linkage point in the labyrinth of underground passageways, which define the below of the entire Giza Plateau, known in ancient Egyptian records as "Rastaw"—the land of tunnels.

In an interview I read from his site, Dr. Hawass claims: *"I found inscribed in the ground the hieroglyphic word 'pr,' meaning 'house.' It is known that the Giza plateau was called 'pr wsir nb rstaw,' or 'the house of Osiris, Lord of Rastaw.' 'Rastaw' refers to the underground tunnels, and most likely the name of the plateau reflects the tunnels inside the Osiris Shaft."*

I couldn't believe Zahi Hawass was finally admitting that the underground of Giza was riddled with tunnels! I knew I had to get in there and see this so-called "tomb" for myself.

The first occasion presented itself to me a little over a month ago. I was in Egypt doing some final exploring and photography for the book when my dear friend Ahmed Fayed advised me that a higher-up in the Department of Antiquities had granted me permission to descend into the shaft.

I was sipping coffee with Ahmed the day before, gazing out at the Giza Plateau from a shisha bar in the village of Nazlet El Samman when, almost out of nowhere, the inspector appeared and they started rambling away in Arabic together. Ahmed introduced me and told him that I was writing a book about the secrets of Egypt, which is about all Ahmed knew about this work.

"What secrets do you know?" the inspector asked, in a slightly dismissive tone. No doubt he was thinking that the authorities are the ones holding the secrets of Giza.

I looked him squarely in the eyes.

"They wouldn't be secrets if I told you, would they?" I replied, teasingly. I took another sip of my coffee.

"Everything depends on what I am allowed to see.. . ." I added, feigning indifference.

"And what do you want to see?" he replied.

Leaping at the unspoken invitation, I told him I wanted to see the Osiris Shaft, which until then was relatively unknown to the world. Only Zahi Hawass himself had openly discussed it in the media.

The inspector told me no one ever goes into the shaft and that it was "forbidden" to enter there. Then, in the same breath, he said: ". . . but of course there are ways around the rules."

Another door opened. Ahmed took his lead and moved into action to negotiate the price and, before I had finished my coffee, the inspector promised entry the next day.

I was quite naturally excited and filled with anticipation, never taking into consideration that we were talking about a life-threatening climb down a twelve-story ladder; never considering what strange bacteria or even stranger energies might be lurking there—deep in the dark—lain dormant for God knows how many millennia.

After breakfast, I was escorted onto the Giza Plateau grounds, to be met by the inspector and taken immediately to the entrance of the great shaft. He told the guard to open the gate, and I was joined by one of the junior archeologists who was to oversee my descent.

Once I got near the shaft, I was consumed with overwhelming emotion and more than just a moment of considerable doubt as to what I was planning to take on.

Determined to face the fear, I walked past the gate and over to the edge of the shaft. I peered over the roughly cut sandstone edge, where the ladder led to the first tier. I steadied myself as I climbed onto the ladder, which descended a relatively short distance (compared to the other two levels) of about twelve feet onto that first landing, where I had to then proceed to a second death-defying ladder... into the deep abyss the ancient Egyptians had mysteriously hollowed out, who knew how many tens of thousands of years before. *See Frame 24.*

Having made it to the first landing, I stared into the bottomless chasm of this interminable shaft and the distance I would have to descend (and eventually climb back up) on the unconvincing steel ladder. I tried to overcome the dizziness of vertigo and residual fear... but I just couldn't do it. The thought of the climb down these widely spaced rungs of rusty metal, so deep and so far, only to reach yet another landing, whereupon I would be faced with another enormous climb down, was too overwhelming. And then, I thought as I stared into the deep, even if I could have made it down the remaining distance... how in the name of Osiris would I have made it back up?

I threw a coin down from the first landing and waited to hear it hit bottom, but I never did. That convinced me. It was farther than I could go... way, way deeper than I dared climb without ropes and other climbing gear.

I stood there, torn between the realization of how rare and magical such opportunities truly are, and the simultaneous realization that it would be sheer insanity to make the descent. As the inspector waited for me to literally take the leap of faith, I briefly contemplated that there would be greatness in leaving this lifetime in such a chamber, falling through the shaft and landing on the incredible and utterly inexplicable sarcophagus, buried thirty-three meters below. There would be worse ways to go, to be sure, than passing to the otherworld through the hidden tombs of ancients.

I inched my way cautiously over to the precipice, resolute, determined, and grabbed on to the handles of the ladder, knowing one false step would mean a straight shot to my death. I was about to climb on, when my mind flashed to the memory of Hatetsesheti . . . the tomb . . . the shaft . . . the darkness.

Knowing how thought manifests in reality, I tried to clear my mind of death and disaster, to focus, instead, on the magnificence of what was truly unfolding before me.

I stepped back over the first rung on the ladder and raced back to the first ladder, shooting back up to safety like a rocket, never feeling the trembling in my legs and never looking back. Although the adventurer within me knew this might be my one and only chance to just possibly enter the Hall of Records (a passageway into another dimension—who knew?), I acquiesced to that ancient fear, once distant and forgotten, now coalescing in the vaporous waters of subconscious mind.

The immediate danger was past . . . but that primordial fear lingered on.

Reluctantly, I thanked the inspector for the chance of a lifetime and walked away from one incredibly rare opportunity to boldly go where, most likely, only a handful of men has ever gone before.

After that traumatic day at Giza, I began having rather nightmarish dreams about it. In these nightly "out-of-body" journeys, I would secretly climb down to the very bottom of the deep shaft, out of sight of the officials, and then be unable to make it back up into the light of day. No one would know I was there, calling to be rescued, and in each dream I would wake up in a fit, coughing, struggling to breathe.

I knew I had opened the proverbial Pandora's box years prior with the regressionist and that this discovery at Giza was somehow part of that experience, playing out in 3D. I realized that I would have to go in, facing this trauma, once and for all.

"It was a shaft . . . it was a tomb," it was the story of Hatetsesheti happening again, in real time.

Just days before completing this book, I was given a second chance to face my dragons and take myself down into the lost inner world of ancient Egypt.

In the short time span between these two most recent visits, I had time to reflect on that fear and work through it, knowing that, if life were presenting such occasions to me, opportunities fellow seekers only dream of, then no doubt I was meant to retrieve and clear the memory from my psyche in order to move forward . . . up the spiral.

I walked the path that led from the Sphinx toward the Great Pyramid and crossed over the sand to meet the inspector, who had come back to accompany me into the shaft. This time, when he turned the key and I saw the gate open once again, I was ready . . . I was convinced . . . and I was sure.

Eager to know and experience what we are all imagining and hoping we will find buried below the sands of the Sahara, I braved the deep of this incredible shaft and committed to taking myself down the treacherous descent.

Facing the fear of that place and time . . . facing the fear of ancient shadows, I stepped over the ledge, climbed down the first ladder to the first level, and then stopped.

The guide joined me at the first-level tier and, when I was ready, he helped me prepare for the next step.

My camera strapped onto my back, I then climbed onto the second ladder, slowly, determinedly, taking care with the meticulous placement of each foot, knowing that one slip of my Adidas and I would, indeed, end up crashing full body into the sarcophagus at the bottom of this endless tube of darkness.

To attempt to describe the powerful energies and force fields that permeate every level of this space defies the limitations of language, but I can tell you that getting to the bottom, there where the granite box lies in the watershed of the beneath, was an utterly supernatural experience. I leave you to imagine what sheer intensity one might feel thirty-three meters below the Giza Plateau: confined in such a small space, the physical body aching from the climb down; muscles contracting and cramping; the adrenaline rushing; the lack of oxygen; the discomfort of the intense heat and humidity; the fear.

At first, all of this physical discomfort was amplified by the conditions of the place, but it soon paled before the wonder of it all—the immensity of what I had accomplished by taking myself to the utter center of the underground at Giza. *See Frames 25A and 25B.*

There, like some secret time traveler, I had left the tourist-filled surface world at the Giza Plateau and was crawling down into the secret lands of an Egypt long forgotten.

The thought of how incredibly blessed I was to have been given such an opportunity drove me on, overcoming the fear and the struggle, as I forced myself to go deeper still.

"Here I am," I marveled, "at the center of something so colossal I have yet to understand it. I am entering the City of Tunnels beneath the Great Pyramid—so close to the Hall of Records I can almost taste it."

In what seemed to be an eternity, I finally reached the last rungs of the ladder that led to the bottom, which was flooded over, just like the Osireion at Abydos. Was it Hakim's mystical Nir River, seeping into the below? Planks formed a walkway over the chamber, but they looked unsafe, and, as spaced as I was, I didn't dare attempt to walk them.

Who knew what unsavory organisms might be breeding in those waters? The last thing I intended to do was fall in!

I hung on to the perilous ladder for life, knowing that I was as close as I had ever been to unveiling some great mystery that has driven me to keep searching, climbing through passageways, locking myself into temples, risking my life to get just a step closer to the illusive truth about our true immortality and our ancestral connection to the stars.

What was buried there, in the shadowy waters of the deep?

I peered into the background to see places where there appeared to be tunnel entrances, but they were hidden behind piles of debris—surely camouflage by the archeological teams who know much more about the underground than that to which we are given access.

The intense heat and humidity of the place were taking their toll and I began to feel light-headed and weak. In an unexpected moment of claustrophobic panic, desperate thoughts of never making it back out filled my mind. I started hyperventilating and almost fell from the ladder into the murky water, as if I were going to actually manifest the earlier thoughts of death at the bottom of the world.

My mind played insane games with me, magnifying my fear the way an oblique light can cast monstrous shadows on the wall. I began hearing strange clicking sounds, like the chelae of scorpions grating against the rocks. Or was it rats, scurrying about in the darkness, just out of my sight?

I held my breath. Silent. I was filled with a very clear sense that I was making contact with the guardians of the space and that my presence there was unwelcome, to say the very least.

I heard what sounded like the hissing sound of a snake.

Terror overcoming me, I managed to speak out into the cavern: "Please forgive me ... please forgive me ... forgive me for invading this place."

It was definitely a snake hissing at me, trying to scare me off.

"I come in the name of the Light, seeker of the ancient secret," I said, speaking to shadows.

The clicking sound stopped. There was utter silence.

I thought about what had given me the courage to descend into this deep, dark place and found strength from that will to know ... to seek. Despite the many emotions—the gripping fear of the unknown; claustrophobia; the threat of unknown guards; panic at the thought of what it was going to take to make my way back out—my mind was incredibly focused. I felt my body, first weak and shaking, now filled with the explosive charge of pure adrenaline.

As I turned full body back to the ladder to climb back out of the shaft, I caught a glimpse of an old man's face, rippling in the still water. It was dark and menacing.

He seemed to be telling me to move quickly and get out.

"You are in the lower Duat, at the second gate," he whispered. "Get out while you can.. . ."

I clutched the rusty ladder and catapulted myself out of there faster than greased lightning, furiously climbing upward, with the single-minded intention to escape whatever spirits guarded the gate, knowing I may very well be fighting unknown warriors for my life . . . perhaps for my very soul.

In the grip of what I saw and heard in the Osiris shaft, I managed to make the climb back to the light of the surface world in record time, despite my wobbly legs and utter exhaustion.

When I reached the first level, the worried guide met me with a bottle of water. He searched my eyes to understand what had happened, but I was so out of breath I couldn't speak, or drink.

I sat on the sandstone ledge, trying to catch my breath.

"Are you all right, Miss Patricia?" he asked.

I poured almost the whole bottle of water over my head, trying to cool down. My breath was desperate and burning.

"Yes, yes," I answered. "I am all right now.. . ."

He looked at me curiously.

"Did you see what you wanted to see?" he asked.

I gazed back over the edge, into the darkness from which I had just emerged.

"I saw beyond that, way beyond what I came to see," I stammered.

My muscles cramping from the climb, I made it up the last few rungs of the ladder from the first tier and returned back to the world I know—the busy Giza Plateau. The sun glared down upon me and I celebrated it as I never have before: the Sun; the Light; the surface world—the land of the living.

As I sat there, drinking light into my being, I thought to myself: "Any closer, and I will find myself on the other side, looking back, just like the priests at Abydos."

Like some last-minute life review, which the dying describe as their "entire lifetime" passing before their eyes, the whole story of my life as the ancient Egyptian Hatetsesheti, flashed before me: my death; the pain and the passing through the gates of the Duat; the longing for the world beyond—the stars...Where Pharaohs Dwell.

It was a moment of absolute realization.

Climbing down into the shaft, reaching this incredible ancient chamber, and making it back into the light of the above, just steps from the Great Pyramid of Giza, was, of itself, a reenactment of the transition from death, to the Halls of Learning, and back: the Osiris Journey.

~ 16

The Screaming Mummy

Months passed.

In July of 2007, I was in Phuket, Thailand, on business, lounging in my sumptuous beachfront suite, after having enjoyed a fabulous spa massage and Jacuzzi session, which the Thais do to the hilt. Snug in my luxurious hotel bathrobe, I floated back to my room and decided to treat myself to a lazy evening in bed. I contemplated watching a movie, ordering room service, and making an early night of it, as I had a full schedule of meetings and interviews the next day.

I was as near to bliss as I had been in a long time, having treated myself to a day of rest, pampering, and total self-indulgence, in one of the world's most breathtaking five-star spa resorts.

Channel surfing the satellite stations of the hotel TV network, I was excited to find that a program I had been longing to see, *Secrets of Egypt's Lost Queen*, was about to begin. It was a Discovery Channel documentary that promised, at long last, to reveal the mummy of Hatshepsut, which, until then, had escaped discovery and remained hidden to archeologists throughout millennia, from her time of rule during the Eighteenth Dynasty of Egypt.[9]

---

[9]According to the Egyptian historian Manetho, her reign lasted twenty-two years, from 1479 to 1458 BC.

I had learned of the show earlier that month but had not expected to have the opportunity to see it air, as I was traveling extensively through Southeast Asia at the time. I should have known, at that point in my Egyptian experience, that Pharaoh Hatshepsut would not elude me and that my travels would not be an obstacle to witnessing such an important revelation as that promised by Zahi Hawass and his team of archeologists, scientists, and investigators.

I ordered dinner to be sent to my room and settled in to enjoy the hour, hoping that the program would offer more than just a Hollywood-style reenactment of Hatshepsut's days of reign, and that it would provide me new insights into my now favorite Egyptian monarch.

The program was centered around investigations made the previous year, when Dr. Hawass and his team had set out to locate and to hopefully identify the mummy of Queen Hatshepsut, from among unidentified mummies stored in the Egyptian Museum. It involved full forensic examinations of four still unidentified, royal family female mummies, believed to be of the New Kingdom: one had been found in a tomb known to archeologists as "DB320" next to Deir el-Bahri, one from tomb KV35 in the Valley of the Kings, and another two (KV60-A and KV60-B) from tomb KV60 in the Valley of the Kings.

Dr. Hawass was convinced that one of the four had to be the mummy of the renowned and controversial Pharaoh-Queen and he declared as much, as I recall, at the opening of the program, stating, in his now famously dogmatic style, that he had found the "proof" linking one of the mummies to Hatshepsut.

Room service arrived right at commercial break: perfect timing.

As the program unfolded, Hawass explained how he had negotiated with Discovery Channel executives that, as terms of their permission to film the groundbreaking story and in consideration of their request for exclusive rights, they would be required to donate a CT scanner to the museum, which would be necessary for the Department of Antiquities to perform the detailed forensic investigations of the mummies. They agreed. Apparently, this was the first time the Egyptians had ever performed such examinations and now, thanks to their collaboration with Discovery Channel, they had been able to set up a forensic laboratory in the basement of the Egyptian Museum.

Hawass and his team of experts subjected the four unidentified mummies to both CT scans and DNA testing, hoping that enough information could be gleaned from the process to provide some proof of a genetic link to other members of Hatshepsut's family lineage, already recorded in data collected by the Department of Antiquities.

I watched, enthralled, as he made his case for identification by process of elimination, whereby he ruled out three of the four candidate mummies and eventually announced that the team had found absolute proof of Hatshepsut's identity.

Dr. Hawass presented a sealed wooden box that had supposedly been stored in the museum, upon which was inscribed Hatshepsut's name. It had been found in DB320, leading to much speculation as to the identity of the mummies that had been found there. It had apparently never been opened, a resinous covering protecting its secret until then.

Passing the mysterious box through the CT scanner, the team identified a mass—some sort of material they believed most likely to be visceral matter (liver and part of the intestines), embalmed and stored in the box, which had then been sealed in its protective coating.

Part of the ancient process of preparing the mummy for burial did indeed involve removing the soft tissue of the body, but it was the rule that, for royalty and nobility, these remains were always placed and stored in elegantly carved alabaster jugs—the famous "canopic jars."

If, indeed, the material inside the box was the liver and intestines of Pharaoh Hatshepsut, it certainly appeared that she most likely had been denied a burial worthy of nobility of the highest order.

The scan also exposed a smaller, more distinct form, very dense matter, which was identified as a "molar." The excitement was palpable, as we know that dental matter is vital to the field of forensic analysis, in that it doesn't break down with time. Dr. Hawass called in one of the leading dental experts in Cairo to assist in examining the tooth and the jaw of the mummy he believed was that of Queen Hatshepsut.

One can imagine how excited they all were when they discerned that this tooth was a perfect match to the jaw of mummy KV60-A, as the jaw was, indeed, missing a molar, and the tooth that was found was apparently an exact fit.

That connection between the molar and the jaw of the mummy KV60-A seemed to convince Hawass that he had broken the silence of Hatshepsut's secret and found the missing pharaoh.

The camera zoomed in to the mummies that had been tagged as "Unknown Woman D" and "Unknown Woman A," revealing first Unknown Woman D, from tomb KV35. Her tests had shown her to be an older woman, older than Hatshepsut's estimated age at her death. The CT scan revealed that Woman D had originally been positioned in the traditional royal pose, her arms crossed on the chest, confirming to Hawass that she had to have been of royal lineage but, given the estimated age at time of death, he deduced it could not be that of Pharaoh Ma'atkara.

Fascinated, I sipped my glass of wine, my eyes glued to the screen.

In that moment, as he went on to describe the second mummy, Unknown Woman A, from tomb DB320 next to Deir el-Bahri, the television camera zoomed to the screaming face of a woman whose ancient, withered remains still carried the pain of what can only have been unthinkable terror and a clearly traumatic death. Dr. Hawass discussed how this mummy could not have been of royalty, based upon the position of her body, and therefore she too was dismissed.

The body was twisted and her mouth was wide open, as if, he stated, she had "suffered at death." At that declaration, one emotional thought raced through my mind: that she had died gasping for air, screaming for help . . . buried alive!

The shock and disbelief at the reality of what I was witnessing and the intensity of emotions that were being stirred within me caused me to choke on my wine and I began to cough, violently, as if the wine had gone down my windpipe. I couldn't catch my breath. With the exception of the dramatic experience of the regression, my struggle to breathe was like nothing I had ever experienced before, except for that once—when I'd had the same kind of attack in the tomb of Thutmosis III, at the Valley of the Kings.

The coughing was so fierce that it sent shooting pain from my lungs tearing through my shoulders and chest, with a powerful burning sensation racing through the bronchioles. It felt as if I were having a heart attack and respiratory failure all at the same time.

Through the fit of this attack, the eyes of the screaming mummy stared back penetratingly at me from the screen. First, I saw the tortured mummy, her pain frozen in time; then I saw the face of a dying woman, a face filled with fear and despair. The picture morphed between the two images in flashes: the mummy's face caught in the camera's lens, on the one hand; the wild eyes of the woman, burned into my consciousness through the screen of psychic vision, on the other.

Oh, my God! That face, tortured and abandoned in the dark hours of an unthinkable death, was a picture of **me**—thousands of years prior and so many lifetimes gone.

Despite all logic . . . despite my years of teaching and learning about the tricks the ego will play on the mind . . . I knew, without question, that I was looking at myself in another incarnation—that lifetime, or rather, that time of dying, in ancient Egypt.

As incredible as it was then and as far-fetched as it will sound to the skeptics who will dismiss my story, I **knew** it as much as I know that I live and breathe.

Staring at me from a television screen, halfway around the world from home, I was face-to-face with a former incarnation. Was this Hatetsesheti, "Unknown Woman A," for whom a cruel destiny had ordained that she die, buried alive, in service to Pharaoh Ma'atkara, Queen of Egypt?

Memories flooded in. There were flashes of scenes of great pageantry and beauty, the golden days—and others of dark terror, at the end—when Hatshepsut was murdered. From the highest authority to a shameful death, she was stripped of her noble rights and buried in such a way that her soul essence would remain eternally entrapped within the corpse—never to soar beyond, so that it might take its rightful place (alongside pharaohs who had come before her) in the stars.

Still in my swimsuit from the spa, I ran hysterically out of the room in the dark of night, over the sandy beach, and straight to the water's edge. Without the slightest consideration of the dangers that lurked in the blackened waters of the night sea, I dove blindly into the waves and starting swimming frantically, trying to exhaust myself—to annihilate the terror of the darkest of deaths.

I swam in order not to cry ... to scream ... to disappear.

I swam in order not to feel ... to mourn ... to lose my mind.

I swam in order not to remember the pain.

I swam just to breathe, to force myself to breathe, rhythmically and methodically, knowing that it was a sort of rebirthing: the letting go of ancient days, ancient memories. It was a time of reckoning—the realization of how all the magical signs and synchronicities that had led me back to my sacred Egypt, land of the Khemitians, were mere reflections of my long, long journey through the gates of immortality.

After I swam and swam in the pale light of the midnight moon, until I could swim no more, I realized that I had truly found Hatetsesheti, the key to my own Egyptian past.

Or, perhaps she had found me.

I dragged myself back up to the beach and dug my quivering feet into the warm sand, remembering how many footsteps I had been forced to walk to reach my grave: how hot the sand; how great the distance.

And it is there, somewhere more infinitely indefinable than

the space between a grain of sand and a moment in time, lost and finally found in the royal tombs of the forgotten, that my story ends.

Bibliography

Cori, Patricia. *The Cosmos of Soul: A Wake-Up Call for Humanity*. Berkeley, CA: North Atlantic Books, 2008.

Cori, Patricia. *Atlantis Rising: The Struggle of Darkness and Light*. Berkeley, CA: North Atlantic Books, 2008.

Cori, Patricia. *No More Secrets, No More Lies: A Handbook to Starseed Awakening*. Berkeley, CA: North Atlantic Books, 2008.

Cori, Patricia. *The Starseed Dialogues: Soul Searching the Universe*. Berkeley, CA: North Atlantic Books, 2009.

Cott, Jonathan. *The Search for Omm Sety*. London: Arrow Books Ltd., 1989.

Dunn, Christopher. *The Giza Power Plant: Technologies of Ancient Egypt*. Santa Fe, NM: Bear & Company, 1998.

Hope, Murry. *The Sirius Connection: Unlocking the Secrets of Ancient Egypt*. Shaftesbury, Dorset, UK: Element Books Ltd., 1996.

Mehler, Stephen. *The Land of Osiris*. Kempton, IL: Adventures Unlimited Press, 2002.

Mehler, Stephen. *From Light into Darkness*. Kempton, IL: Adventures Unlimited Press, 2005.

Mehling, Marianne, ed. *Egypt: A Phaidon Cultural Guide*. London: Phaidon Press Limited, 1990.

Omm Sety and El Zeini, Hanny. *Abydos: Holy City of Ancient Egypt*. Los Angeles: LL Co., 1981.

Temple, Robert K. G. *The Sirius Mystery*. Rochester, VT: Destiny Books, 1976.

Vallée, Martine, ed. *The Great Shift*. San Francisco: Red Wheel/Weiser, LLC, 2009.

Acknowledgments

The list of people whose love and support help me be free to follow my path is becoming greater with every step. Souls in so many places around the world, sharing moments of wonder and light, are too numerous to name—but you know who you are. Thank you for your laughter, your spirit, your wisdom . . . and your trust.

I give thanks, above all, to the light beings who forever surround me in their love, illuminating the way. It is such a celebration, and a comfort, to know you are always there. . . .

To Richard Grossinger, who has shown me what it means to work with an ethical and dedicated Publisher, I am filled with gratitude and an experience of collaboration far greater than I could have imagined. Very special thanks to Hisae Matsuda, my editor, for her dedication to perfection and for wading through all the elements and pieces of the puzzle that are presented in the book. To all the people at North Atlantic Books, for putting your hearts to the task of birthing this work, I am eternally grateful.

Special thanks to Debbie Johnson, for her insights into the Simulacra at Deir el Badri, Fred Hageneder, for his illustrations, Metka Lebar, for her fabulous orb at the Osireion, Philippe Ullens, for his photograph of the doorway crop-circle in Wiltshire, and the British Museum, for permission to use their graphic designs of the gods of the Pantheon.

My friends in Egypt, who graciously find the ways to help me walk the sacred lands, are a joy beyond measure. Thanks to my Egyptian brother, Ahmed Abrahim Fayed, handling all my tours and ground arrangements, and his loving family, for always reminding me how Egypt truly is my home. Thanks to Mohammed of the Giza Plateau, for your wisdom and knowledge—and access to secret worlds. To my dear Amir of Abydos, Keeper of the Gates and brother across the sands of time, I owe you so much for all you do. . . . And to everyone at Abydos: Kevin, Nancy, Shahad and all the good people of the village. I am always at home in the warmth of your love and friendship.

To my beloved Hakim, who told me he would be "waiting, on the other side of the tunnel," thank you for being part of my life and much of my inspiration. Stephen Mehler, a wonder who has recently come into my life, thank you for your generosity of spirit and the sharing of your wisdom . . . and to Theresa as well, a sister soul, journeying the same roads to discovery.

And forever, Franco my soul mate, you are the exquisite lighthouse that always guides me home, unconditional love that has withstood the test of time as we recognize it . . . and mysteries—other lifetimes—that we have yet to discover. Together.

Index

Permissions

Illustrations by Fred Hagenader (pages 1, 28, 119, 120, 157, 158), Joel Guilleux, antikiforever.com (page 28), and Christopher Bird (page 130)

Illustrations on pages 74, 75, 106, 108, 110, 111, 112, 114, 145, 146, by permission of the British Museum

Photographs by Phillipe Ullens (page 144); Patricia Cori (pages 168, 171), and Lucy Pringle (page 194)

Tarot card design on page 31 by kind permission of Builders of the Adytum, 5101 North Figueroa St., Los Angeles, CA. 90042; http://www.bota.org/

Disclaimer: "Permission to use Builders of the Adytum images in no way constitutes endorsement of the material presented in this work."

The Last Supper (page 169) Scala / Ministero per i Beni e le Attività culturali / Art Resource, NY

About the Author

PATRICIA CORI is an author, shaman, and spiritual guide to the sacred sites of the Earth. A native of the San Francisco Bay Area, Patricia Cori has utilized her clairvoyant abilities in healing and support work throughout her life, which has been dedicated in great part to the study of mysticism, philosophy, ancient civilizations, metaphysical healing, spirituality, and unexplained mysteries.

She is a prominent figure in the Spirit Movement, well-known on the international lecture circuit—actively offering courses, seminars and workshops around the world on a vast range of topics, which reflect her broad knowledge of alternative methodology in healing and her remarkable gift of helping others rekindle and ignite the power within.

She has been recognized and celebrated as a gifted shaman by indigenous spirit teachers of the Tibetan and Mayan traditions. In 1996, she established the LightWorks travel club, SoulQuest™ Journeys, and that year led a group of spirit travelers, to whom she introduced the sacred temples and breathtaking spirit of the Tibetan landscape, to Nepal and Tibet. For more information, visit www.sirianrevelations.com